The Reel Cowboys
The Real Cowboys

Poems and Art
by
Christine Riker

Return once more to those Saturdays of old
When we watched our Cowboy Heros bold
Do exploits marvelous to be seen,
As they rode across a silver screen.

This is a work of nonfiction biographical and literary commentary. The author made every effort to be accurate and complete and to avoid any copyright infringement and welcomes comments, suggestions, and corrections, which can be emailed to: info@digitalegend.com.

Note: John Wayne used with permission of Wayne Enterprises, LP. The John Wayne Cancer Foundation's mission is to bring courage, strength and grit to the fight against cancer. www.jwcf.org

To contact the author write to:
Far Horizons Art Studio
1516 E 4500 N
Buhl, Idaho   83316

First Printing November 2020

ISBN- 978-1-937735-96-8

Artwork for cover and throughout the book: Christine Riker

DIGITAL
LEGEND

1-801-810-7718
www.digitalegend.com

Dedicated to the memory of all the silver screen cowboys,
both genuine cowboys and actors, who kept the
Western Frontier alive for generations of
boys and girls the world over.

DIGITAL
LEGEND

INTRODUCTION

The "American Cowboy" was unique in the history of the world. No other time period or county produced such an unusual "hero." The Middle-Ages had its "Knights in Shining Armor," but they were the armed forces of the countries and kingdoms in which they lived. They were from the nobility and ruling class of their kingdoms. The American Cowboy was a simple working man, a hired-hand on horseback. The "Cowboy Era" began at the end of the Civil War and lasted until the end of the century. By the 1890s the cowboy had already become a mythic figure, the symbol of individuality and courage. During the war between the states, Longhorn cattle in Texas had multiplied in huge numbers, unattended, while the men were away in military service to the Confederate States of America. The northern and eastern states were in serious need of meat, and the solution to the problem resulted in the great cattle drives to trailhead towns, such as Abilene, Kansas. Cattle trails had names, like the Abilene Trail, the Chisholm Trail, the Pecos Trail, the Bozeman Trail, and the Loving-Goodnight Trail.

Population in the west was sparse. The civilized comforts and refinements of towns were equally sparse. Law enforcement was almost non-existent. Cowboys spent most of their days and nights living outdoors, so they had to be strong and rugged. They had to depend upon themselves and each other for protection, fellowship, and every emergency, so loyalty and honesty were essential elements of the cowboy life. Soon a mystique of romance developed around the cowboy. The result was stories, songs, books, legends, and later, western movies, television shows, and cowboy poetry gatherings which we have today. A simple working man becoming a legendary, heroic figure, was a historic milestone in human history.

With the beginning of motion pictures in the first half of the twentieth century, many men were still alive who had actually been cowboys, and some of them, like Tom Mix, became actors in the early films. From the 1920s until the 1960s, Western movies were a staple in Hollywood, with such memorable films as those made by John Ford, starring the great John Wayne, and stars like Gary Cooper, Randolph Scott, and Joel McCrae. During the early decades of television, the 1950s and early 1960s, half of the TV shows were Westerns. The "Cowboy Movies" of the 1920s, 1930s, 1940s, and early 1950s upheld the tradition of courage, self-reliance, honesty, decency, and purity. The Western heroes wore white hats and villains wore black hats. Good always triumphed over evil. There was no "gray" in between. It was the era of "Hoppy, Gene, and Roy."

Christine Riker

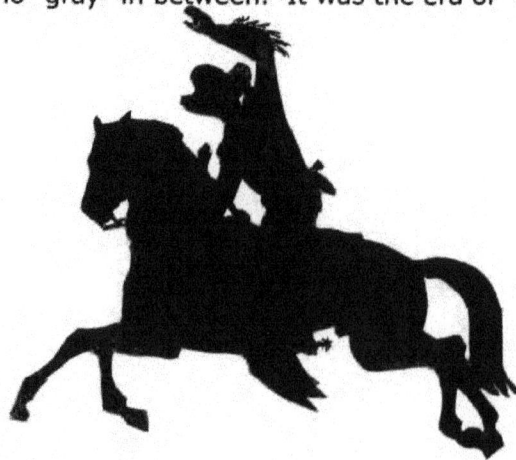

2

CONTENTS

Movie Cowboy Poems, Illustrations, Text, and Photographs by Christine Riker.
Three poems by Audie Murphy - One poem by W.A. Phelson - One poem by John Mitchum.
Permission letter from Wayne Enterprises to publish poems and art of John Wayne.

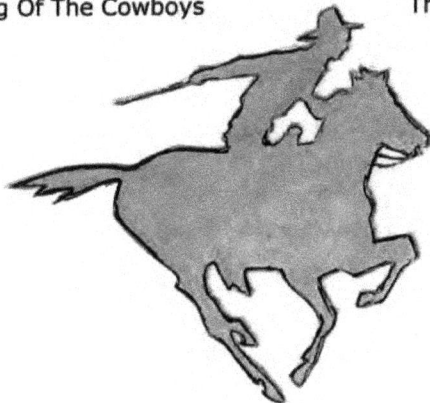

ONCE UPON A SATURDAY

Once upon a Saturday,
    So many years ago,
My brother* and I looked forward to
    The weekly picture show.

With twelve cents for a ticket,
    And a nickel more to spare,
We bought a big red apple,
    To munch while we were there.

We went to see the "shoot 'em up,"
    With a hero tried and true,
Who rode the range of yesteryear,
    Beneath a sky of blue.

He always had a special horse,
    As smart and strong as he,
And a funny friend called a side-kick,
    As faithful as could be.

They roamed the West together,
    And vanquished every foe,
Fought renegades and rustlers,
    Wherever they would go.

If a comely Miss was in distress,
    Or any kind of need,
Our cowboy hero saved her,
    With utmost haste and speed.

Father, brother, ranch, or town,
    He to their rescue came,
Their plight resolved without reward,
    Of pay or praise or fame.

For virtue was its own reward
    For our cowboy hero bold,
Who rode the range of yesteryear,
    On Saturdays of old.

* Mickey Tyrone

by Christine Tyrone Riker - 10-19-2003

4

The King Theater during the 1950s.

The old theater building in 1988.

The theater in Gorman, Texas, where Mickey and I watched Hoppy, Gene, and Roy during 1939, 40, and 41. It opened as the New Deal Theater in the 1930s. It was named in honor of Franklin Roosevelt's New Deal program instituted in 1933. It was renamed King Theater around 1942. By 2009 the building was being used as a Senior Center.

MADE IN AMERICA

The tragic war between the states had ceased,
It was time for a nation to mend,
For men who had worn the blue and the gray,
To face one another as friend and friend.

On the remote and rugged Texas plains,
Longhorn cattle ran wild and free,
Untended throughout the years of war,
Vast herds as far as the eye could see.

Confederate currency but worthless paper,
No money at all for the necessities of life,
Southerners and Texans faced a bleak future,
Until recovery occurred from the recent strife.

People up north and in the east needed meat.
Beef was plentiful in the Lone Star State,
Getting them together was the problem at hand,
Finding a solution seemed indeed, quite great.

In the nick of time railroads pushed their way west,
While cattle-trails sprang from the Texas soil,
The Goodnight-Loving, the Western, and Chisholm,
Blazed by men toughened by grueling toil.

Just a hired hand, a hard working man,
Who did his job from the back of a horse,
This quirk of fate did a legend create,
And American history changed its course.

With a hat to shield his face from the sun,
A kerchief to protect from the alkali dust,
While riding drag behind the moving herd.
To protect from thorns, boots and chaps a must.

He seemed set apart from a man on the ground,
Slowly plodding behind a mule and a plow,
Or a shopkeeper in an apron, behind a counter,
Or a bespectacled businessman mopping his brow.

The "Cowboy" was fictionalized in story and song,
In the lurid dime-novel and Wild West Show,
Like the 101 Ranch's and Buffalo Bill's,
Thus he became famous wherever he would go.

With the advent of film and motion pictures,
He was the pioneer who led the way,
"The Great Train Robbery," the first feature film,
Only 12 minutes long, a Cowboy classic to this day.

We should give honor where honor is due,
To the real cowboys whom we've never seen,
And those who entertained us, Saturday afternoons,
The movie cowboys of the silver screen.

Many there were before my time and yours,
Beginning with the silent screen days,
To the era of sound when shots could be heard,
From Colt six-shooters and rifles ablaze.

Our thanks we give to one and all,
Please forgive if we've missed anyone.
The legend of the "Cowboy" was made in America,
Whether real or reel, he was America's favorite son.

By Christine Riker - 8-9-2019

WHERE GOD PUT THE WEST

Western movie fans of the early days,
    Came to know the scenery so well,
If a road or rock or tree was out of place,
    Boys and girls in the theater could tell.

The B-Westerns were usually filmed around Hollywood,
    On the Corrigan Movie Ranch, and Vasquez Rocks,
In the Alabama Hills in Lone Pine and Bronson Canyon,
    And on sets built on the studio's back-lots.

Rarely did a studio leave Hollywood to go on location.
    With "The Vanishing American," starring Richard Dix, in 1925,
Followed by "Trader Horn" in 1931, starring Harry Carey, Sr.,
    Filmed in Arizona and Africa, location-filming did survive.

When we think of "The West," these scenes come to mind,
    The canyons of Moab, Utah, with their wide open spaces,
Oak Creek Crossing, AZ, the 19th century train in Jamestown, CA,
    Saguaro cactus around "Old Tucson," AZ; these are the places.

But our imaginations turn first to Monument Valley, AZ,
    Its flat plain, mesas, and spires, were an awesome mixture,
Often called "John Ford and John Wayne" country because,
    As a location for their films, it almost became a fixture.

Neither man was the discoverer of that enchanted land.
    In 1920, Harry Goulding was allowed to build a trading post,
When the only way into the valley was on horseback or on foot,
    A remarkable gesture by the Navajo, his very gracious host.

During his early trips into that valley, he had helped the Navajo
    Prevent a shooting war with the neighboring Paiutes.
In gratitude, they had allowed him to homestead a small piece
    Of reservation land, out among the monuments and coyotes.

With his new bride, nicknamed "Mike," and a few sheep, he built
    A trading post at the foot of a mesa called "Big Rock Door,"
The only privately held land in the 25,000 square-mile reservation,
    The Navajo homeland, now his and Mike's home, forevermore.

With his last $60, a bedroll, and photos of his valley, Harry journeyed
    To the Hollywood studios. What happened next is no mystery.
In 1939, John Ford made "Stagecoach," starring John Wayne,
    And the rest is, as they say, "Hollywood history."

By Christine Riker 8-28-2019

Harry Goulding

Mike Goulding

9

THE DRUGSTORE COWBOY

He stopped short in his tracks to stare,
    This old cowpoke with graying hair,
He'd never seen anything quite so strange,
    As this flashy dude, since he left the range.

With rough, gnarled fingers he rubbed his chin,
    And his leathery face broke into a grin,
Then a belly-laugh shook him down to his boots,
    And he split the air with hollers and hoots.

He looked this gent over from his head to his toes,
    An' guessed him a tenderfoot from the cut of his cloths.
With his battered old Stetson he slapped his thigh,
    And wiped a mirthful tear from a faded blue eye.

The weathered old waddie wore a chambray shirt,
    And his run-down boots were covered with dirt,
Levis covered his lean, hard flanks,
    And leather chaps circled his bowlegged shanks.

The drugstore cowboy, on the other hand,
    Was dressed like a dandy in cloths quite grand,
Neither wrinkle nor dust could mar his looks,
    A modern day idol of movies and books.

They were both cowboys in an odd sort of way,
    But one was real and one was "play."
For the man imprisoned by civilized ways,
    Still longs for the freedom of "Cowboy Days."

When trust and strength were the measure of a man,
    And freeways and fences didn't slash the land.
To cowboys all, both the wishful and true,
    For preserving the West, we are grateful to you.

By Christine Riker - 12 - 15 - 2003

Chris Riker

TIM HOLT

Tim Holt was the man with the boyish face,
    So winsome, young, and sweet,
And when he starred in the shoot-'em-up,
    We knew we were in for a treat.

Chito, as Richard Martin was called,
    Rode faithfully by his side,
Through twenty nine films in the golden age,
    Of Hollywood's Western pride.

They trounced the villains, swift and sure,
    As Western heroes should,
And in their hands the right prevailed,
    As we all knew it would.

It made our week feel quite complete,
    As off to the theater we'd go,
To spend our Saturday afternoons,
    With Tim Holt at the picture show.

By Christine Riker - 12-25-2006

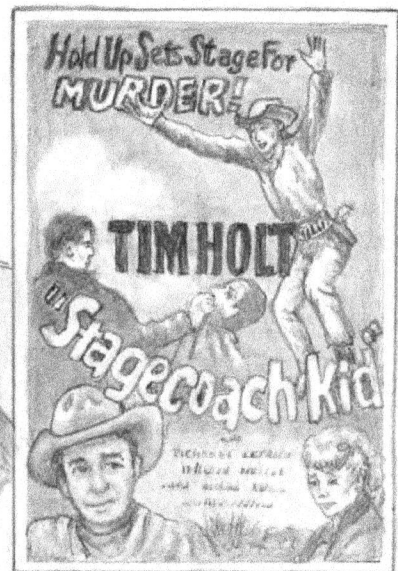

RANDOLPH SCOTT   1

His voice was as soft as thistledown,
And he spoke with a gentle ease,
Honeysuckle accented words as faint
As perfume on an evening breeze.

An actor of note, his profession was,
Southern gentleman his character spoke,
He rode into our hearts on the back of a horse,
As a rugged and noble cowpoke.

Whether hero of epics of World War Two,
Or quintessential Western man,
His elegant face on the silver screen,
Won many a devoted fan.

Tall in the saddle and proud he sat,
Hero to our generation,
Whose forebears had in days long past,
Moved west and built a nation.

Handsome of face and manly of form,
He portrayed our distant past,
On a favorite mount named Stardust,
In movies where he was cast.

Long may his Western films survive,
So he can ride another day,
On yesterday's range in memory,
May he never fade away.

By Christine Riker 12-25-2006

Chris Riker

He was as handsome of face and perfect of form,
As any man could possibly be,
With a soft Southern drawl, his baritone voice,
Completed the man we had come to see.

A Randolph Scott Western to thrill young and old,
A story unfolding upon the silver screen,
Unlike silent reading from the pages of a book,
This story could both be heard and seen.

He held his own when starring with John Wayne,
And Errol Flynn, or starring alone on the screen,
In ninety-seven fine films spanning three decades,
This tall, rugged actor was a romantic dream.

An exciting way to end an ordinary week,
On Saturdays of old, in a time gone by,
A treasure to store in our memory banks,
We fondly recall Randolph, with a smile and a sigh.

By Chris Riker 8-9-2019

Chris Riker

Actors Lee Marvin and Don Barry have words with Randolph Scott in "Seven Men From Now, " 1956

Randolph Scott was born Randolph Crane on Jan. 23, 1903, in Orange county, Virginia, into a family who were among the first settlers in Virginia. He was educated at Woodberry Forest Prep School, Georgia Tech, and the University of No. Carolina, to be an engineer. While visiting in Hollywood, he came to the attention of Howard Hughes , who introduced him to Cecil B. De Mille. He enrolled at the Pasadena Playhouse, and the rest is, as they say, history. His movie career spanned 1929 to 1961, while remaining one of the top box-office draws in the world.

Randolph played in 97 films, of many genre, but is best remembered as one of the greatest Western stars. He was a gentleman on the screen and in private life.

CHARLES STARRETT

Back when I was just a kid,
    Many long years ago,
Homework and play was what we did,
    And we went to the Saturday picture show.

We always saw a "shoot 'em up,"
    My brothers, cousins, and friends,
And watched a hero in a big white hat,
    Bring bad men to their ends.

A cowboy hero who rode that range,
    Was handsome as could be,
Tall and athletic, with flashing dark eyes,
    Charles Starrett was one we went to see.

On his trusty horse named "Raider,"
    He rode to the rescue time and again,
To save a damsel in distress,
    Or to help a needy friend.

He often played "The Durango Kid,"
    On the silver screen, so long ago,
And taught us how to live with honor,
    At our weekly Saturday picture show.

By Christine Riker 2-8-2015

Charles Starrett was the star in over 130 Westerns. He was born in Athol, Massachusetts, 03-28-1903.

Charles Starrett was born on March 28, 1903 in Athol, Mass. He was president of the dramatic club in his prep. school, Worcester Academy. At Dartmouth he became known as an outstanding athlete, also winning a scholarship to the American Academy of Dramatic Arts. He aspired to be a serious actor, but settled for a career as a cowboy star, beginning with bit parts in 1926. His career as a cowboy star began when Columbia Pictures chose him to take over for the late Colonel Tim McCoy and Buck Jones in Westerns. His first picture was "Gallant Defender" with Leonard Sly, who later became Roy Rogers. Starrett was an excellent horseman and his movie horse was "Raider." He was known to be pleasant to work with. After seventeen years with Columbia Pictures, he retired. He was a founding member of the Screen Actors Guild, holding the tenth membership card ever issued. He married his childhood sweetheart and they had twin sons and two grandchildren. They lived by the Pacific Ocean in Laguna Beach, CA

17

THE OWENS VALLEY COWBOY

He crooked his leg over the saddle horn,
    Gazed in wonderment and awe,
At the valley floor before him,
    And the strange goings-on he saw.

Where yesterday cattle grazed in peace,
    Searching for tender young grass,
Beneath the wild and pungent sage,
    On sand as yellow as brass.

The flat plain hummed with activity,
    Men with cameras moved in and out
Among the boulders and the monoliths,
    Barking commands with a profane shout.

Cameras rolled, reflectors beamed
    The light to shadowed places,
Make-up artists rushed to powder
    Handsome, chiseled faces.

Cowboy actors rode about,
    On silver mounted saddles,
Burnished horses pranced in and out,
    Amid furious outlaw battles.

The Owens Valley cowboy,
    With a grin on his rugged face,
Slowly withdrew a sack of Bull Durham,
    And rolled a smoke at a leisurely pace.

He shook his head in amusement,
    That the Alabama hills should hold,
Studio crews where once there camped,
    Prospectors who searched for gold.

He slowly turned his cowpony,
    Toward the sunset in the west,
And rode straightway into history,
    A cowboy hero we all love best.

By Christine Riker 2-14-2006

THE ALABAMA HILLS

In the Year of Our Lord, 1863,
     With our country in battle array,
The Northern boys in jackets of blue,
     Faced Southern boys in gray.

In California's rocky hills,
     Far from their Southern home,
Digging for golden nuggets there,
     A band of miners did roam.

Stories reached their lonesome ears,
     Exploits of a cruiser came,
Which was raising cane in the Yankee fleet,
     The ALABAMA was her name

So they named their mining claims for her,
     In tribute to her fame,
And that is how the Alabama Hills,
     Came by their unlikely name.

By Christine Riker 12-24-2006

Bob Steele

Johnny Mack Brown

Saturday-matinee
Western heroes
of the
1930s & 40s

Born Robert North Brandbury, Jr. on Jan. 23,1906 in Pendelton, OR. He began films at age 14 with a twin brother, Bill. He became a cowboy star in 1927, in spite of his small size. His father, Robert Bradbury, Sr. was head of MONOGRAM Studio. Perhaps that did help a bit. He appeared in 150 films, both A and B movies.

Johnny Mack Brown was born on Sept. 1, 1904, in Dothan, Alabama. He was a football star and Rose Bowl hero in 1926. He entered films in 1927, starring in 200 movies, both A and B films. He acted for all the major studios, and retired in 1953. He was an exception to the usual rule: White hat...good guy. Black hat...bad guy.

Joel McCrae was born in So. Pasadena, CA, Nov. 5, 1905. He entered the movies as a stuntman in the 1920s and began his performing career in 1929. He acted in every genre, and was known as a "dependable performer" with an "everyman" image. His performances were low-keyed and his personality

Chris Riker

likable. He began his Western period in 1946 with "The Virginian," and remained with Westerns the rest of his career, becoming one of the most beloved Cowboy stars of all time. In private life, he was married to film star, Frances Dee, since 1933, and they had three sons. They owned ranches in Southern California.

LONE PINE

Way out in the Owens Valley, 'long about half-way down,
Nestled at the foot of Mt. Whitney, is a little, high-desert town.

Unless the lone traffic signal should slow you down a bit,
You'd pass right through the place and never notice it.

But in times gone by, its glory days, it was a mighty bustling place,
A town where make-believe and reality, met daily face-to-face.

Movie companies roamed about, out in the Alabama Hills,
Filming scenes of daring-do, of chases, spills, and thrills.

There outlaws robbed stage coaches, rustled cattle by the score,
Shot it out with posses, across the sandy desert floor.

There Saturday matinee idols bunked at night in the Dow Hotel,
Played poker to pass the time away, when rain stopped filming for a spell.

Out on the Spainhower-Anchor Ranch, on the southern edge of town,
Was Hopalong Cassidy's favorite haunt, where he took the outlaws down.

They say Tombstone was too tough to die, for its villains and heroes bold,
Who defined the West on a raw frontier, in those lawless days of old.

But who kept the American West alive, so all the world would know?
It was the Hollywood movie makers, with their Saturday picture show.

They brought their crews to Lone Pine, where the Western got its start,
Way out in the Owens Valley, in the town with a Western heart.

By Christine Riker - 2-14-2006

OFF TO LONE PINE

As Summer bids farewell to all,
     And the days turn into burnished Fall,
The folks who love our Western lore,
     Are off to visit Lone Pine once more.

There to meet with friends of old,
     And remember cowboy heroes bold,
Whom we admired in bygone days,
     For their courage and their honest ways.

We come by plane and bus and car,
     Hoping to see a movie star,
Who worked in the cowboy films of yore,
     And walk down memory-lane once more.

Poets and musicians are there as well,
     Movie producers with a story to tell,
Indian maidens and dance-hall girls,
     With jet-black braids and golden curls.

Good guys and villains in white hats and black,
     Horsemen and stuntmen, we nothing lack,
Forums and movies and chuck wagon meals,
     To the echoes of hooves and wagon wheels.

Through boulders and rocks in canyons deep,
     Where twenty-mile shadows in evenings creep,
On location tours we get to go,
     Where once they filmed our picture show.

So, we're off to Lone Pine once again,
     To meet new folks and long-time friends,
To honor the people whose exciting ways,
     Brightened our youthful, halcyon days.

And when the week-end draws to a close,
     We say, "So long," and everyone knows,
As we wave good-by to one and all,
     We'll see one another in Lone Pine next Fall.

By Christine Riker   3-11-2007

TRIBUTE TO A SON OF THE WEST

Once upon a time there lived a man,
    Who truly loved the West,
The vanished one of years gone by,
    But the "reel" one he loved best.

For the cowboys of the silver screen,
    Were his heroes when a boy,
And he longed to be like all of them,
    Like Hoppy, Gene, and Roy.

When he was grown he traced their steps,
    Through canyons deep and wide,
Among the boulders scattered there,
    Where outlaws used to hide.

High adventure was for him,
    To find the very spots,
Where camera crews of long ago,
    Filmed their famous shots.

So great was his enthusiasm,
    For the lore of the silver screen,
It must be shared with one and all,
    Be felt and heard and seen.

He gave his talent, time, and self,
    In museum, festival, book, and art,
Through video films and tours as well,
    Flowed the fervor of his heart.

Along the sandy streets of Lone Pine and
    Out in the Alabama Hills,
Where twenty mile shadows fall at dusk,
    Those memories are living still.

Listen closely and you may hear,
    The heroes he loved as a boy,
Dave Holland now rides side by side,
    With Hoppy, Gene, and Roy.

by Chris Riker
7-7-2006

A WESTERN LEGEND

From a matinee idol of the silent screen days,
To the golden-age of Hollywood stars,
An unlikely western hero emerged from book to screen,
Who rode the range on a horse before the day of cars.

A middle-aged hero with pre-mature white hair,
And clear blue eyes as cold as steel,
With his crew of Bar-20 comrades in tow,
He dealt frontier justice, bringing outlaws to heel.

The first movie I can remember seeing,
When I was a lass just six years old,
Was William Boyd playing Hopalong Cassidy,
With his Bar-20 crew, riding brave and bold.

He upheld righteousness and protected the weak,
Chased rustlers and outlaws, withstood all the ills,
Which plagued the wild and lawless frontier,
Out among the rocks in the Alabama Hills.

He became a legend in his own time,
Along with the beloved Gene and Roy.
They were model heroes to be emulated,
By every American girl and boy.

Long may their memory live in our hearts,
To show us the way when we go astray,
To "have the right stuff" from the very start,
As we each live our lives, day by day.

By Christine Riker 8-7-2019

William Boyd as Hopalong Cassidy and James Ellison as Johnny Nelson of the Bar-20 Ranch

HOPALONG CASSIDY

If memory returns to serve me well,
    (And I'm never quite sure it does)
There's a little story I'd like to tell,
    Of a time that really never was.

Of a time on Saturday afternoons,
    In those easy bygone days,
Of batwing doors on smoky saloons,
    And wild and wooly ways.

When movie cowboys rode a range,
    Spread across a silver screen,
Whose deeds and dress were awfully strange,
    On a bona-fide range were never seen.

Hopalong Cassidy, the first of the breed,
    I saw when I was a child.
He rode upon a stalwart steed,
    And spoke with a drawl, gentle and mild.

And often riding by his side,
    To give a dash of humor sly,
Was dear old side kick, Andy Clyde,
    With quizzical expressions, blank and wry.

In those early films the horses fled,
    In jerky leaps and bounds,
Twenty feet each step they sped,
    As if chased by Satan's hounds.

My *brother believed, (yes, I must tell)
    That Hopalong got his name,
Because his horse could hop so well,
    It earned him lasting fame.

However that character came to be,
    In those days so long ago,
It brightened childhood for *Gene and me,
    At the Saturday picture show.

*Gene Tyrone, my brother

By Christine Tyrone Riker - 8-24-2008

Actors Charles Middleton, playing "Buck Peters," and William Boyd, playing "Hopalong Cassidy," on the Russ Spainhower ranch, doubling for the Bar-20, near the Alabama Hills, Lone Pine, CA, the setting for the first in the series of "Hoppy" films, made in 1935.

CLARENCE E. MULFORD'S
"Hop-a-long CASSIDY"
WILLIAM BOYD JIMMY ELLISON

PAULA STONE
GEORGE HAYES
KENNETH THOMPSON
ROBERT WARWICK

The Alabama Hills scene from the original lobby card set of the first "Hopalong Cassidy" movie in 1935, filmed in Lone Pine, California.

Chris Riker

HOPALONG CASSIDY

"Hoppy" was a character created by a mild-mannered, bespectacled civil servant named Clarence Edward Mulford, who lived in a modest apartment in Brooklyn, New York. He spent his spare time writing about the mythical western frontier, which was so different from his real life. He created the literary character, Hopalong Cassidy, and his Bar-20 crew. The first Hopalong Cassidy story, "The Fight at Buckskin," appeared in the December 1905 issue of "Outing Magazine." In the summer of 1935, the first Hopalong Cassidy movie was filmed in Lone Pine, California, out among the rocks in the Alabama Hills and on the Russ Spainhower Ranch. Russ supplied the horses, cattle, and equipment for western films made there, for many decades. There were 66 feature films and 52 TV episodes of the Hopalong Cassidy series produced during the era of the Westerns. Screen star, William Boyd, was so identified with the fictional character, that no other actor was ever used to portray him. Thus, a modern western legend was born.

THE CISCO KID

In old California appeared a man,
　　　Straight from O Henry's pen,*
To champion justice swift and sure,
　　　To lure the reader in.

Onto the movie screen he rode one day,
　　　To delight the audience there,
With Pancho riding by his side,
　　　He rescued maidens fair.

His steed was decked in silver rich,
　　　So was the Cisco Kid,
As shining in the morning sun,
　　　As the valiant deeds he did.

He righted all the wrongs he met,
　　　Before he rode away,
With Pancho riding by his side,
　　　To return another day.

On the little screen which came along,
　　　Now his story could be told,
To generations yet to come,
　　　Of that Robin Hood so bold.

To give a lesson needed sore,
　　　To youngsters sitting there,
Just how to be a hero's friend,
　　　And treat all people fair.

With lighthearted salutations,
　　　He bid us remember when,
Heroes fought the villains vile,
　　　And triumphed in the end.

*William Sidney Porter (1862-1910)

By Christine Riker
12-25-2006

Leo Carrillo was born August 6, 1880 in Los Angeles, California, on land which his ancestors had owned under Spanish rule, before the Americans took possession. A graduate of St. Vincent of Loyola, he was a newsman and cartoonist before becoming a dialect comedian in vaudeville and later on the legitimate stage. Entering films in the late 1920s, he became one of Hollywood's busiest character actors of the 1930s and 40s, at first playing leads, but later typically providing comedy relief as an amiable Latin. In the early 1950s, after retiring from the big screen, he played Pancho, Duncan Renaldo's sidekick, in "The Cisco Kid" television series.

**

Duncan Renaldo's date of birth is uncertain, but thought to be April 23,1904, and his birthplace is also unknown, but thought to be Spain. He was a foundling and never knew his parents. He passed away in 1980. He was reared and educated in various European countries and arrived in the U.S. in the 1920s, as a stoker on a Brazilian coal ship. Failing to succeed as a portrait painter, he entered films as a producer of shorts, later signing on as an actor with MGM in 1928. The studio capitalized on his Hispanic looks to type him as a Latin lover in a few late silent films and early talkies. He was briefly imprisoned in 1932 on immigration charges. He returned to the screen and played leads and supporting roles for various studios, mainly for Republic. By the 1940s, he found his niche in Westerns as one of the Three Mesquiteers, and in the middle of the decade, became the star of his own Western series, playing "The Cisco Kid," the fourth actor to play that part. The series was popular and in the early 1950s it became a television staple, with Duncan still in the lead. During his film career, he played in a large variety of films, including "The Lone Ranger" and "Zorro" series. He co-starred with Harry Carey Sr., in the 1931 film, "Trader Horn," the first movie to be filmed on location, which was set in Africa. Noteworthy, the female star of that film, Edwina Booth, shot to stardom with the role of a white goddess in a black tribe, but quickly disappeared from public view the next year. The studio gave a rumor that she had died of a jungle fever contracted in Africa. Apparently she developed a lifelong illness from the experience and retired from the screen. Fortunately, neither Harry Carey Sr., nor Duncan Renaldo suffered any ill effects from their time in Africa, so audiences were able to enjoy their performances on the screen for many more years.

ZORRO

The Lone Ranger wasn't the first Cowboy star to wear a mask,
Strange though it may seem...our "heroes" wearing masks!
Disguises should be used only by outlaws to hide their identities
As they go about their dastardly deeds and crooked tasks.

The early "talkie" Western hero, Ken Maynard, once wore one,
In a Saturday matinee movie called "The Cattle Thief," in 1936.
That topsy-turvy wardrobe shenanigan added a bit of mystery,
Used by the Lone Ranger and Zorro, it enhanced their bag of tricks.

The Latin hero Zorro, was played by extremely handsome men,
Douglas Fairbanks, Sr. in 1920, with his unique swashbuckling style,
Followed two decades later, in 1940, by Tyrone Power, so charming,
Then Zorro was added to television Westerns after a suitable while.

Walt Disney added Guy Williams to the role, in his movie in 1957,
Which developed into a television series and ran for three joyous years.
Such an intriguing hero can't be allowed to disappear, therefore,
Zorro returned in 1990, with Duncan Regehr, amid applause and cheers.

Zorro was an early Western hero, hidden behind a black cape and mask,
In Spanish California in the 1820s. Don Diego De La Vega was the son
Of wealthy land-owner, Don Alejandro. By day playing a foppish fool,
But secretly by night, riding his black horse, "Toronado" quietly on a run.

Swiftly going to the aid of the downtrodden peasants, his neighbors,
Paying crushing taxes, under the oppressive heel of Captain Monastario.
Keeping his secret from the Dons who were tyrannized by the Captain,
And his true identity known only by his trusted man-servant, Bernardo.

The Pueblo De Los Angeles was the wicked Captain's base of operations,
Hidden securely from the authorities and rulers in far away Spain,
Until the courageous, masked defender finally liberated the Peons there,
Making Old California a beautiful and happy place to live, once again.

By Christine Riker 9-21-2019

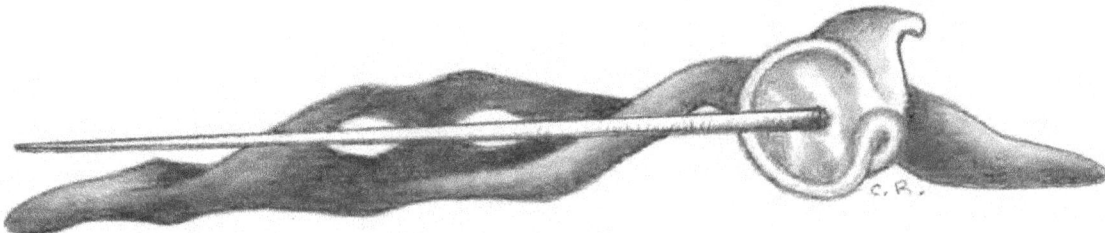

Douglas Fairbanks, Sr.
1920

Tyrone Power
1940

Guy Williams
1957

Duncan Regehr
1990

chris Riker

ZORRO, was based on a story by Johnston McCulley, called "The Curse of Capistrano."

After the initial movie industry moved from the East Coast to the sunny climate of Southern California, and Hollywood became the movie-making capital of the United States, it seemed logical that films celebrating the Spanish inspired hero, known as Zorro, would be produced. The heroic character was based on a story by Johnston McCulley, "The Curse of Capistrano."

The first Hollywood "Zorro" was played by actor Douglas Fairbanks, Sr., born Douglas Elton Ulman, on May 23, 1883, in Denver, Colorado. He was the son of a prominent Jewish lawyer and a Southern belle, who was raised by his mother from age five, after their separation. She resumed the name of her first husband, which was "Fairbanks," thus Douglas was given his surname. Douglas made his stage debut at age 12 in local plays. They moved to New York in 1900 and he made his debut on Broadway in 1902. By 1910 he was an established star. In 1915 he was lured to Hollywood, where he became the screen's most beloved hero. He displayed such cheerful exuberance, moral courage, a devil-may-care-attitude, and such physical agility, that he became the prototype of the idealized image of the American male. During a WWI Liberty Bond tour with Charlie Chaplin and Mary Pickford, he and Mary fell in love and were married in 1920. They reached the peak of their success during the 1920s. He was as popular in early tongue-in-cheek comedies as he later became in swashbuckling adventures. In 1929, his stage-trained voice allowed him to make a smooth transition to sound, but he was growing older, and in 1936 he announced his retirement from acting. In December, 1939, he died of a heart attack in his sleep.

The next Hollywood "Zorro" was the very handsome Tyrone Edmund Power, Jr., who was born May 5, 1913, in Cincinnati, Ohio. He was a superstar during the 1930s and 1940s, the "Golden Age" of Hollywood. The son of matinee idol, Tyrone Power, Sr., he went on the stage when in his teens, playing bit parts. He became a major box-office asset of 20th Century Fox in 1937, during a career which was interrupted when he joined the service at the start of WWII. He starred in many of Hollywood's best movies during his career, both as a dashing, swashbuckling hero, and in dramatic roles. He also acted on stage after WWII. He was married to actress Annabella from 1939 to 1948, and to actress Linda Christian from 1949 to 1955. He died of a heart attack in Madrid, Spain, on November 15, 1958, at age 45, during the filming of the movie, "Solomon and Sheba."

Later-day "Zorros" included Antonio Banderas in the movie, "The Mask of Zorro" in 1998, as well as television shows starring Guy Williams in 1957, and Duncan Regehr in 1990, proving the masked Hispanic hero is as enduring as story-telling has always been, and always will be.

Douglas Fairbanks, Sr.   Tyrone Power, Jr.

Up in Lone Pine, California, where hundreds of Western movies, as well as movies of other genre, were filmed, beginning in the 1920s, Dave Holland and Terry Powell started the Lone Pine Film Festival in 1990, to pay tribute to the movies made in Lone Pine and the Alabama Hills, and to preserve the movie locations in that area. In addition to the unique rocks of the Alabama Hills, the Anchor-Spainhower Ranch where so many of the Hopalong Cassidy films were made, and the surrounding area which contains a lake and expanses of sand, stand the majestic Sierra Nevada Mountain Range as a backdrop, with Mt. Whitney looming in the distance.

ZORRO to the rescue of Chris Riker, who was visiting Lone Pine when they showed up.

ZORRO and citizens of the Pueblo De Los Angeles, show up in Lone Pine, CA, just in case the residents of that small community need to be rescued.

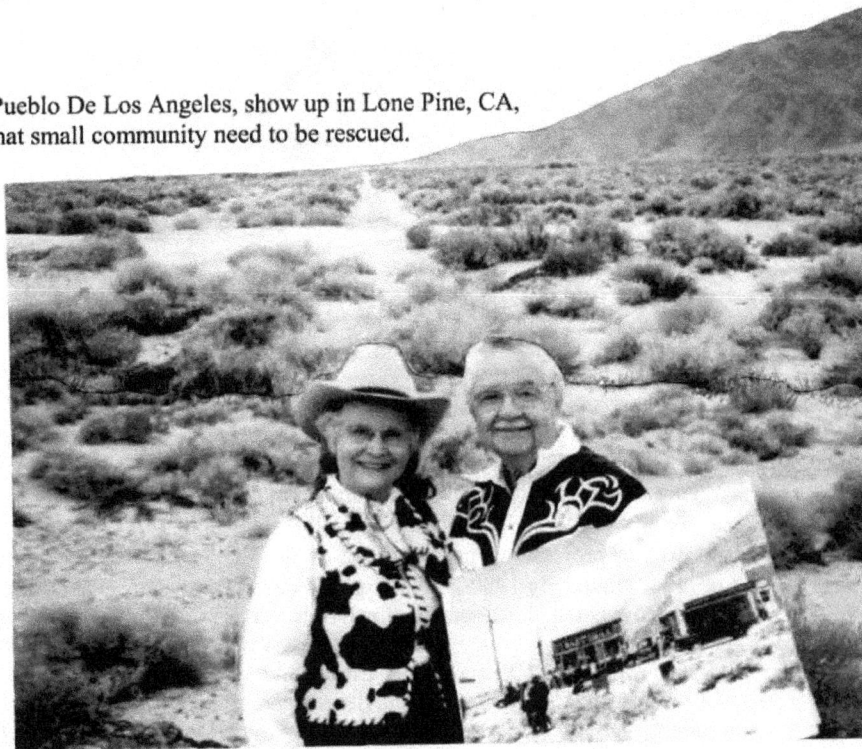

Chris Riker and Dave Holland are standing at the site of the town built for the movie, "Bad Day At Black Rock," starring Spencer Tracy. The site is at the north-eastern edge of Lone Pine.

WILLIAM ELLIOTT

When I was just a lass, my brother and I used to go,
On Saturday afternoons to see a moving-picture show.
Shopping was the way Mom and Dad spent the day,
And visiting with other parents, they whiled the time away.

One of our favorite cowboy heroes, whom we often saw,
Was handsome William Elliott. He was fast on the draw,
And whether portraying Wild Bill Hickok or Red Ryder,
He was just as handy with his fists. He was a great fighter.

He had the most unusual side-kick of any Western actor,
A winsome little Indian boy, an important factor.
Wearing a great big feather, carrying arrows and a bow,
He came to the aid of Red Ryder, wherever they did go.

They rode the range together, the boy and the man,
To show us, one and all, that our Creator had a plan,
So our parents, our teachers, and our friends all would know,
We learned to be true-blue, at the Saturday picture show.

By Christine Riker -11-14-2004

William Elliott was born Gordon Elliott in 1903, in Pattonsburg, Missouri. A former rodeo competitor, he made his screen debut in 1925, playing mostly supporting roles in non-Western films under his real name. He even played the villain in a Gene Autry film under his name, Gordon Elliott. After appearing in a serial for Columbia studio, "The Great Adventures of Wild Bill Hickok" in 1938, he adopted that character's name as part of his new professional name, adding "Wild Bill" to Elliott. He went on to star in many Westerns of the 1940s and early 1950s, including the "Red Ryder" and "Wild Bill Hickok" series. I saw him in person in 1961 when he headlined the local rodeo in Sonora, California. He passed away just four years later, in 1965. In 2004, in Lone Pine, California, I met Ronnie Aycoth, a re-enactor from South Carolina, who looked very much like William Elliott, and enjoyed playing the part, to keep the memory of that popular movie star alive. The Western movie heroes of the Golden Age of Hollywood gave us more than just entertainment.   They gave us a moral code by which to live and thrive. Choose good over evil. If we heed the code they left us, our nation will have a chance to survive and to have a future.

BILL ELLIOTT, aka "WILD BILL" HICKOK

"Folks call me Wild Bill, but I'm really a piece of a man,"
    To my childish ears he seemed to say,
Spoken by Bill Elliott as "Wild Bill" Hickok,
    At the Saturday matinee.

He looked quite whole to me, as far as I could tell,
    A handsome man, slender and tall,
Dressed as a 1940s cowboy with two six guns,
    Holstered backward, to top it all.

No sooner had those peaceful words been spoken,
    Than violence erupted on the screen,
With thrashing fists he subdued the villain,
    And the triumph of justice could be seen.

After time had flown and I was grown,
    With years of history tucked in my head,
It occurred to me, as an afterthought,
    Just what he had actually said.

He'd spoken the words, "I'm really a peaceable man,"
    Though Hickok's reputation belied that fact.
He was brought to life as a Western hero,
    By Elliott's acting skill and tact.

For those of us, who in childhood days,
    Grew up with the Western men,
Give thanks to Ronnie Aycoth for bringing back
    Bill Elliott to thrill us once again.

by Christine Riker - Nov. 14, 2004

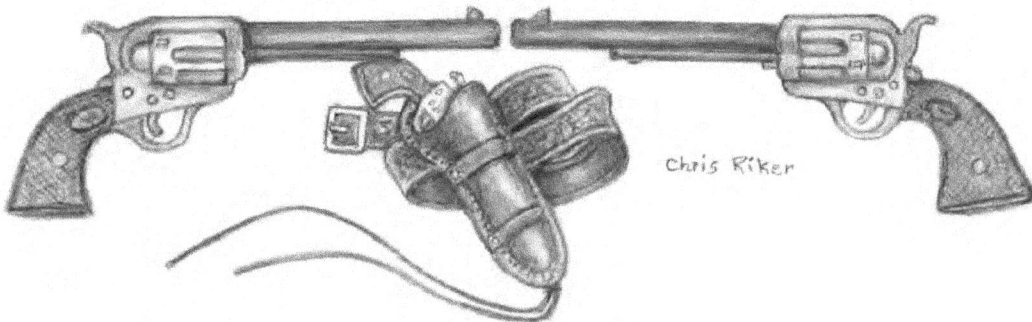

Chris Riker

Honoring the Memory of "Wild Bill" Elliott

I saw Bill Elliott in person, in Sonora, California, Sunday, May 14, 1961, Mother's Day, which was also my son Kerry's birthday, when Elliott was the headliner at the annual rodeo. I had only seen him in the movies as "Wild Bill Hickok," but never saw him as "Red Ryder."

Ronnie Aycoth as RED RYDER

Ronnie Aycoth and I became friends in October 2004, when I met him and other Western movie re-enactors in Lone Pine, CA

THE LONE RANGER

He wasn't winged Pegasus, but he came close,
    His mane in the wild wind blowing,
With a "Hi, Yo, Silver," and away they sped,
    As smooth as quicksilver flowing.

He carried the Masked Man far and wide,
    Each Saturday morning for years,
On the radio in our front room,
    For adventure they had no peers.

With Tonto his faithful companion,
    They fearlessly faced each danger,
And together the friends rode side by side,
    The Indian and the Lone Ranger.

The stirring strains of a melody,
    The overture to "William Tell,"
Bid us come away each Saturday,
    Drawn by its luring spell.

Into the West we longed to share,
    With our wild imaginations,
To roam the canyons and prairies wide,
    In exciting situations.

Where we would ride with the Masked Man bold,
    Facing each mortal danger,
And with a silver bullet we
    Would triumph with the Lone Ranger.

"Hi, Yo, Silver," and away they rode,
    Into history's countless pages,
The Masked man and his Indian friend,
    Belong to the timeless ages.

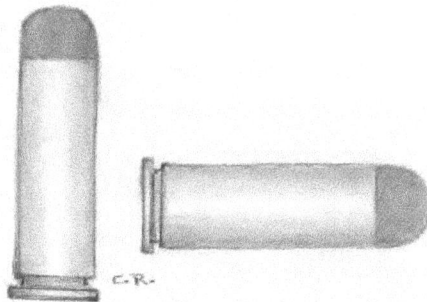

By Christine Riker 12-26-2006

Clayton Moore as The Lone Ranger
Jay Silverheels as Tonto

THE LONE RANGER AND TONTO

The strains of the "William Tell" overture began to play,
    Then a haughty "Hi, Yo, Silver, and away,"
Came booming from the radio in the front room,
    On Saturdays of old, which seem just yesterday.

When a company of Texas Rangers were ambushed,
    Only one Ranger was left alive,
Was it luck, or fate, or something more,
    Which decreed this one man would survive?

Chosen by the Divine Creator for a purpose,
    To bring justice and order to a lawless land,
With a loyal Indian friend to ride by his side,
    Wherever he was needed, to lend a helping hand.

He rode a magnificent white stallion called "Silver,"
    And wore a mask to hide his handsome face,
With Tonto, his companion, on his Indian pony,
    Helping the distressed, traveled from place to place.

People have always been drawn to stories,
    Whether children or seniors, aged and old,
Repeated by memory, down endless generations,
    In books or films, however they are told.

The story of this latter-day knight, the Lone Ranger,
    And his faithful Indian companion, Tonto, too,
Have inspired generations by now, and will continue,
    If, to their ideals, we followers will remain true.

By Christine Riker 9-21-2019

Clayton Moore was born September 14, 1914, in Chicago, Ill. A former circus aerialist and male model, he entered films in 1938, performing stunts and playing bit parts until 1942, when he began playing lead roles. He played in action pictures and played villains as well. He is best known as "The Lone Ranger "in the TV series and its two feature films.

Jay Silverheels was born Harold J. Smith, May 26, 1919, on the Six Nations Indian Reservation, Ontario, Canada, the son of a Mohawk chief. He was a famous lacrosse player and amateur boxer before entering films in the mid-1940s. He played supporting roles in numerous pictures and gained fame on TV in the role of Tonto, first John Hart's, than Clayton Moore's "The Lone Ranger." He was in the two films of "The Lone Ranger." In 1974 he started a new career as a harness racing driver.

THE SINGING COWBOYS

There came a time when saloon brawls and horse chases,
And a posse cutting the outlaws off at the pass,
Could become a bit repetitious for the audience,
So songs were included, to add a bit of class.

Now Saturday matinee audiences were serenaded,
With melodies and songs so lovely and clear,
And music-loving parents could join their kids,
For a musical concert they could both see and hear.

Believe it or not, the first "singing cowboy" was John Wayne,
In an "oater" as a hero called "Singing Sandy."
It was not John Wayne you heard warbling out his heart,
To leading lady, Cecilia Parker, sitting nearby so handy.

Robert Bradbury Sr., head of the studio, had two sons,
One was Bob Steele, a B-picture cowboy star.
"Singing Sandy's" voice was supplied by the other,
But it failed to advance Wayne's career very far.

We can thank John Ford for giving John Wayne the role,
Of The Ringo Kid, in "Stagecoach," his classic Western story,
A new star was born, and a 30-year era of top-quality Westerns,
With Yakima Canutt's hair-raising stunts, in their spectacular glory.

Then, genuine musicians and singers entered the picture,
And gave us decades of memorable music and song,
As well as riding and fighting, handling Winchesters and Colts,
While putting outlaws and villains in jail where they belong.

They were all handsome and athletic and physically fit,
Just as heroic, leading men in those days had to be,
Gentleman, pure in heart and speech, generous and kind,
Role-models to imitate in life, for youngsters like you and me.

Who can ever forget Gene Autry, his gentle, handsome face,
His sweet singing voice so melodious and fine,
In between songs he rode the range on Champion,
Bringing villains to justice, keeping outlaws in line.

We all loved Roy Rogers, the King of the Cowboys,
And his golden palomino, the wonder-horse named Trigger,
With Dale Evans by his side, to movie stardom he did ride,
Rodeos, records, movies, and TV, fame and family grew ever bigger.

Tex Ritter was a historian's treasure-trove in song,
Forever linked to the 4 Academy Award winning "High Noon,"
Known more for his music than his many movie films,
And his son, comedian John Ritter, who died too soon.

Lesser known were others who graced the silver screen,
Sang just as well, and also never lost their hats in barroom brawls.
Rex Allen with his beautiful brown Morgan named Koko,
And Eddie Dean, who rode so many horses, you couldn't name them all.

We tip our Stetsons to the singing cowboys, one and all,
With their songs, their horses, and their funny side-kicks too,
Who entertained us so pleasantly when we were young and small.
Their valiant fight for justice taught us right from wrong, as we grew.

By Christine Riker - 8-10-2019

America's first singing-cowboy movie actor was none other than John Wayne. He was "Singing Sandy" in an early B Western, "Riders of Destiny." Problem was, John Wayne couldn't sing. Robert Bradbury, head of Monogram studio, had two sons; Bob Steele, a Western cowboy star, and the other son was a doctor or dentist, according to movie critic Leonard Maltin. The "other son" had a great singing voice and it was his voice which was dubbed for Singing Sandy. His name was Smith Ballew, according to John Wayne biographer, George Bishop. Wayne served a 10 year apprenticeship in B Westerns for Monogram and Mascot studios, learning how to be "John Wayne," while also doing bit parts for major studios. Then, another young singing cowboy appeared in Hollywood, starring in B Westerns. He had a beautiful voice, as well as being handsome. His name was Gene Autry. He quickly became the favorite singing cowboy of the movies. Together, John and Gene were instrumental in the merger of Monogram and Mascot into a new studio. It was Republic. John and Gene made the first two films Republic produced.

Born Marion Michael Morrison, May 26, 1907 in Winterset, Iowa. Died June 11, 1979.

***

Tex Ritter was born Woodward Maurice Ritter, Jan. 12, 1905, near Murvaul, Texas. He died in January 1974. Cowboy star, Grand Ole Opry star, recording artist and folk hero, and the only entertainer elected to both the Cowboy Hall of Fame and the Country Music Hall of Fame. He collected southwest folklore and cowboy ballads while studying political science at the University of Texas. He dropped out of Northwestern University's law school to begin a folksinging career on radio and on stage. In 1930 he was on Broadway and in 1936 made his debut in films. In the 1940s he took to the road with his horse, White Flash, in live shows, often with his side-kick, Slim Andrews and his mule, Josephine. In 1941 I saw Tex, Slim, and Josephine on stage in the movie theater in Gorman, Texas. White Flash didn't make an appearance that afternoon. Tex sang the title song, "High Noon" for the movie of that name in 1952. In 1970 he made an unsuccessful bid for the Republican nomination for US Senator from Tennessee. Too bad, as he would have been a great senator. His wife was actress Dorothy Fay. Their son John was the star of TV's "Three's Company." In his Western movies, he sang genuine cowboy ballads which he had collected over his lifetime. He was a genuine cowboy as well, saying he learned to ride a horse before he learned to walk. He was a genuine Western singing cowboy hero of the silver screen. May his memory long endure.

Gene Autry was born on September 29, 1907, on a ranch near Tioga, Texas. He died Oct. 2, 1998. While working as a railroad telegrapher at a junction in Oklahoma, the great Will Rogers heard him sing and encouraged him to go into show business. In 1928 he started singing on a local radio station, and three years later starred in his own radio show and made his first recordings. In 1934 he made his first screen appearance, singing in a Ken Maynard Western, "In Old Santa Fe." This led to his first starring film, a 13-chapter serial, "Phantom Empire," followed by a feature film, "Tumblin' Tumbleweeds." in 1935. With his comic side-kick, Smiley Burnette, and his horse, Champion, he made dozens of Westerns for the Republic Studio.

During WWII, Gene Autry served as a flight officer with the Air Transport Command. During his absence, a young man named Roy Rogers inherited the rank of Republic's "King of the Cowboys."
***
Roy Rogers was born Leonard Sly on Nov. 5, 1912 in Cincinnati, Ohio. He died July 6, 1998. Arriving in California in 1929, he worked as a migratory fruit picker. He entered films in 1935, and the rest is history.
***
Were there any cowgirl singers? Yes...one! Dale Evans, born Frances Octavia Smith on Oct. 31, 1912, in Uvaldi, Texas. She died Feb. 7, 2001. A nightclub and radio singer, she reached Hollywood in the 1940s, and married Roy Rogers on Dec. 31, 1947, becoming the "Queen of the West," both in their movies together, and the popular TV series, "The Roy Rogers Show."

Monte Hale...Born June 8, 1921 in San Angelo, Texas. He was the last great singing cowboy star of Republic Westerns of the cowboy classic era. He made an easy transition from singing at rodeos and vaudeville shows to movie stardom. He headlined 29 films between 1946 and 1950. Tall in the saddle at six ft. 5 in., he always got the girl after rounding up all the bad guys. His genial good looks, accomplished guitar playing, and melodic voice made him an audience favorite. He passed away on March 29, 2009.

Rex Allen...was born December 31, 1922, in Wilcox, AZ. Rex started his career in vaudeville, then sang on radio and starred in a traveling rodeo show, before becoming a singing cowboy of Republic Westerns. His side-kick was often Slim Pickens and his horse was Koko. Later, he starred in the TV series "Frontier Doctor," and narrated and sang in several Walt Disney movies, such as "Charlie, the Lonesome Cougar" and "The Legend of Lobo." He also narrated the animated film, "Charlotte's Web." He passed away December 17, 1999.

Eddie Dean...born Edgar Dean Glosup, date unknown, but possibly in 1910, in Posey, Texas. He was a singing cowboy star of Hollywood films of the 1940s. He began his career as a Western singer on the radio in 1930, and started playing bit parts in films in 1936. Eddie reached peak stardom in the mid-1940s when he was among the top ten most popular cowboy stars, but soon afterward, retired from films. He passed away March 29, 1999.

Best known of the singing cowboys was the first to become famous, Gene Autry, followed by Roy Rogers.

The song most associated with Gene Autry, is "Back In The Saddle Again," written by Gene and Ray Whitley.

Leonard Sly performed with several musical groups with very little success, until the mid-1930s, when he teamed up with Tim Spencer and Bob Nolan, forming the Pioneer Trio. They performed on a Los Angeles radio station, KFWB. One afternoon, Harry Hall, the announcer, introduced them as The Sons of the Pioneers, explaining to the startled trio afterward, that they were too young to be pioneers, hence "the sons of..." The name stuck, and the group with the smoothest harmonies and best wistful western sound became the most famous of all the Western movie bands.

At times, the Sons of the Pioneers consisted of Leonard Sly (Roy Rogers), Bob Nolan, Tim Spencer, Pat Brady, Lloyd Perryman, Ken Curtis, & Karl and Hugh Farr. Bob Nolan wrote "Tumbling Tumbleweeds."

BOOTS AND SADDLES

"Back in the Saddle Again," a song which music lovers and movie fans
Will always associate with movie cowboy, Gene Autry, as his theme song,
Just as "Happy Trails" will be remembered as Roy and Dale Rogers' song.
Gene Autry was the first genuine "Singing Cowboy" who came along.

Gene was born before the real Western frontier had faded totally away,
In 1907, on a ranch near Tioga, Texas, as any real cowboy should be.
While working as a railroad telegrapher in Oklahoma, a man heard him sing,
And encouraged him to go into "show business." Will Rogers, that was he.

In 1928, Gene began singing on the radio; in three years had his own show,
And he was recording hit songs, among the more than 200 he had written.
He made his first film appearance in 1934 in a Ken Maynard film, then starred
In a 13-chapter serial "Phantom Empire," and by the movie-bug was bitten.

With his trusty horse, Champion, and comic sidekick, Smiley Burnette,
His Westerns were packed with action and song; his romances very few.
He was a no-nonsense hero; then came the chance to be one in real life,
As a flight officer with the Air Transport Command during World War Two.

Among other talents of this handsome man with the sweet and kindly face,
Was a beautiful singing voice and talented skill on his melodious guitar.
He was an astute businessman and was one of the top ten moneymakers
In Hollywood; his common sense and intelligence carried him very far.

He formed a film production company and a radio and television chain.
He had ranches and oil wells, a hotel in Los Angeles, and a flying school,
The California Angels baseball team, and a Western museum in his name.
What an accomplishment for a movie star; he was certainly "no-ones fool."

Gene had a long and productive life, and a spectacularly successful career,
But to the Saturday matinee crowds, to each young girl and young boy,
He was just our cowboy hero, who always came to the rescue when needed,
Our very own GENE, of the favorite Western trio, "Hoppy, Gene, and Roy!"

By Christine Riker   8-24-2019

Orvon Grover Autry, born in the community of Indian Creek, a few miles from Tioga, Texas,
passed away on October 2, 1998, at age 91. On April 1, 1932, after a whirlwind courtship of
two or three days, he married Ina Mae Spivey; then on October 7, 1932, resigned his job with
the railroad to devote full time to his radio and recording career. Ina Mae died in 1980, and on
July 19, 1981, he married Jackie Ellam and continued his business career. His music and show
business career spanned nearly 70 years, he recorded and wrote hundreds of songs, acted in 93
movies, and starred in 91 television productions, a remarkable record for an entertainer!

When I was 7 years old, I saw Gene Autry in person in Jackson, California. He was in town for
the annual rodeo, and was standing on the main street of this old gold-rush town, in front of the
hotel, signing autographs with cedar pencils, which he tossed aside after the signature was given.
My mother kept one of the pencils as a souvenir, because she was a fan of Gene Autry.

Gene Autry gained fame as a singing cowboy, and led the popularity poll of Western stars for several years. He is the only Western star listed among the ten top moneymakers in Hollywood films (1938-1942). On the screen, Autry was a no-nonsense cowboy hero. His films were packed with action. His network radio show had a large following. His recordings sold in the millions. He wrote 200 songs, including "Here Comes Santa Claus." His recording of "Silver Haired Daddy of Mine" was the first record to sell a million copies. He was an astute businessman, who owned a radio and TV chain, ranches, oil wells, a flying school, publishing company, and...

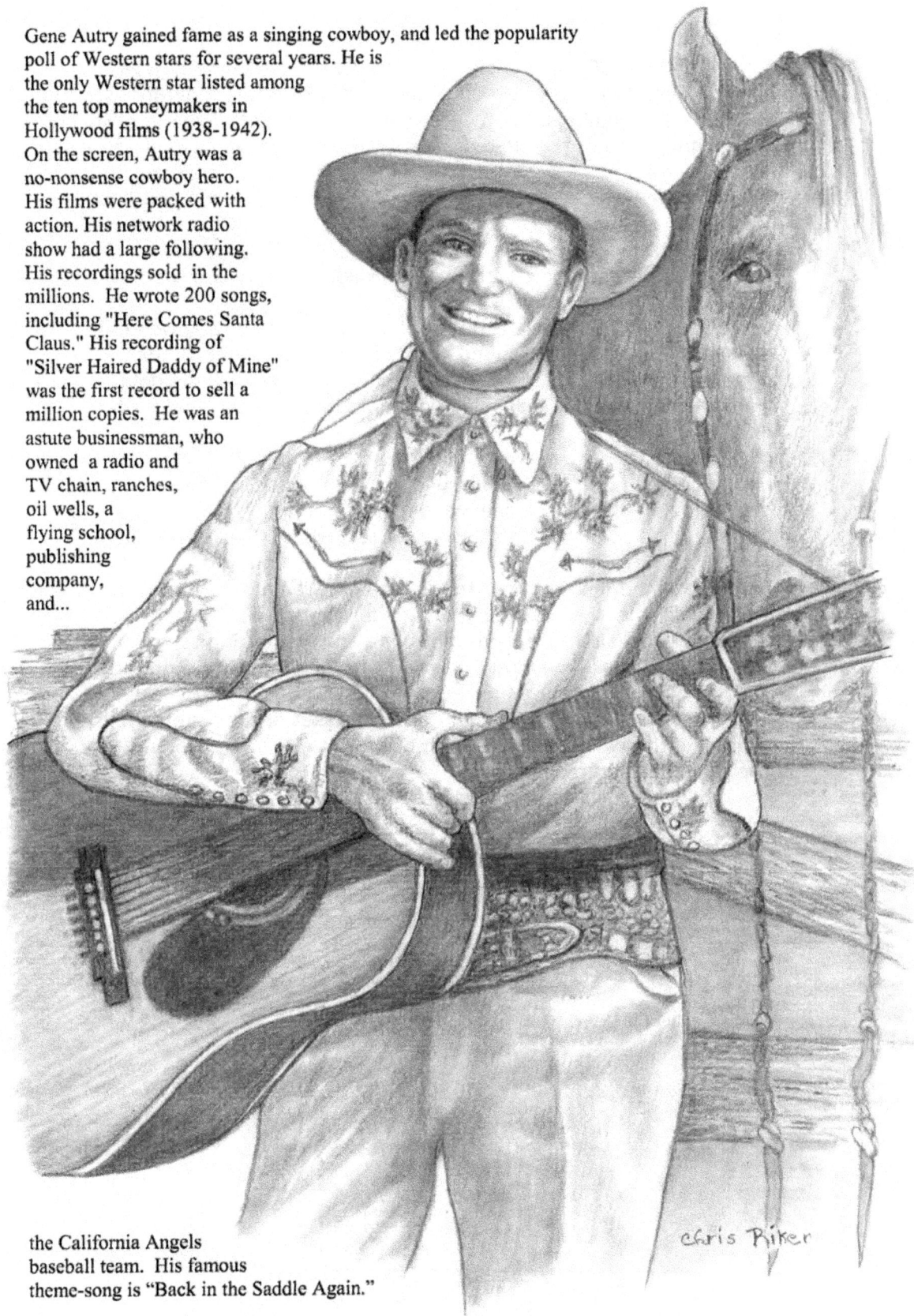

the California Angels baseball team. His famous theme-song is "Back in the Saddle Again."

KING OF THE COWBOYS

Roy Rogers and Dale Evans deserve their titles, most honorably won,
"King of the Cowboys," and "Queen of the West," to three generations,
Born in humble beginnings, he in Ohio, she in Texas, both lived in poverty,
Before reaching fame in the United States, and in multiple foreign nations.

Roy's birth name was Leonard Franklin Sly, only son of Mattie and Andy,
A tentative start, singing with Bob Nolan and the "Sons of the Pioneers,"
And sorrow with the death of his first wife, Arline, at Dusty's birth,
A starving migrant-camp in Southern California, his early trail-of-tears.

She was born Frances Octavia Smith, before marrying her boyfriend,
Thomas Fox, at age 14, and having a son, Tommy, the light of her life.
She had many short-lived jobs as a radio singer and big-band singer,
But making a career alone was filled with hardship, hunger, and strife.

Clearly, Roy and Dale earned the successes they enjoyed later in life,
When they gained fame and popularity, and were world-renowned,
With their singing and music, the wonder-horse, Trigger, famous too,
Children they had born and adopted, and the Christian faith they found.

Their faith gave them strength in the deaths of three of their children.
One was little Robin, who was born and died with Down's Syndrome.
Dale's book, "Angel Unaware," brought hope and inspiration to millions,
Keeping future "Down's" children out of institutions, keeping them at home.

Hollywood will never again see actors and actresses of their high quality,
"The Queen of the West" and the "King of the Cowboys" were one-of-a-kind.
May the struggles and the successes they experienced during their lives,
Become models to inspire future generations, to imitate and to enshrine.

By Christine Riker 8-24-2019

ROY ROGERS
KING of the cowboys
TRIGGER
SMARTEST HORSE IN THE MOVIES
My Pal TRIGGER
A REPUBLIC PICTURE

Roy Rogers, known to millions of fans as the "King of the Cowboys," and his famed Palomino "wonder horse, " Trigger, brought joy to children everywhere. Not only did children enjoy the Western movies, and later, the TV shows of this famous pair, Roy's wife, Dale Evans, and side-kick, Gabby Hayes, but their parents loved the Rogers family as well. They became outspoken Christian leaders, and champions for the rights of orphaned children when they adopted several youngsters of different ethnic backgrounds, to rear along with the daughter and son born to Roy and his wife, Arline, who died Nov. 3, 1946, from a blood clot, after giving birth to Roy, Jr. (Dusty) on Oct. 28, 1946. Roy filled the void with volunteer work at children's hospitals, entertaining terminally ill and handicapped children.

On Dec. 31, 1947, Roy married his leading lady of 12 films they made together. Two and a half years later, Roy and Dale had a daughter, Robin Elizabeth Rogers, born Aug. 26, 1950. Robin had Down's syndrome. Robin died the day before her second birthday, Aug. 25, 1952. Dale turned her grief into a book about Robin, "Angel Unaware," which resulted in Down's syndrome children, thereafter, living at home, rather than being placed in institutions.

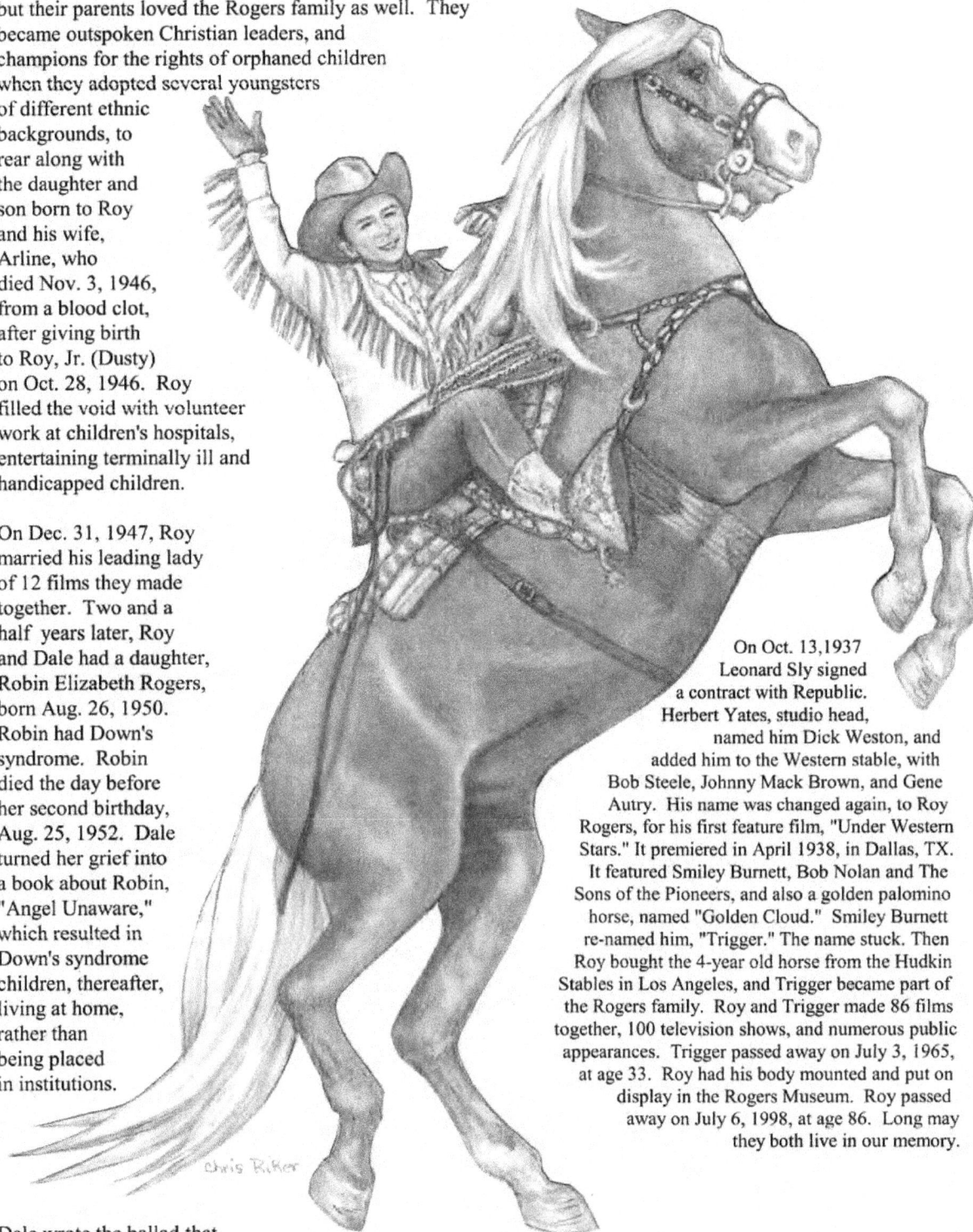

On Oct. 13,1937 Leonard Sly signed a contract with Republic. Herbert Yates, studio head, named him Dick Weston, and added him to the Western stable, with Bob Steele, Johnny Mack Brown, and Gene Autry. His name was changed again, to Roy Rogers, for his first feature film, "Under Western Stars." It premiered in April 1938, in Dallas, TX. It featured Smiley Burnett, Bob Nolan and The Sons of the Pioneers, and also a golden palomino horse, named "Golden Cloud." Smiley Burnett re-named him, "Trigger." The name stuck. Then Roy bought the 4-year old horse from the Hudkin Stables in Los Angeles, and Trigger became part of the Rogers family. Roy and Trigger made 86 films together, 100 television shows, and numerous public appearances. Trigger passed away on July 3, 1965, at age 33. Roy had his body mounted and put on display in the Rogers Museum. Roy passed away on July 6, 1998, at age 86. Long may they both live in our memory.

Chris Riker

Dale wrote the ballad that was to become their theme song: "Some trails are happy ones, other are blue; It's the way you ride the trail that counts; Here's a happy one for you. Happy Trails to you until we meet again..."

JOHN WAYNE

Over rough and tumbled cowboy trails,
    You rode into America's heart,
The long way around in B-Western films,
    You earned your keep and got your start.

Even then, your presence filled the screen,
    Astride a horse, on a pilgrim's quest,
Or riding the restless waves of a sea,
    You gave each role your very best.

As you acted, you grew into the man,
    All the world has come to love,
The rugged individual of the American dream,
    With freedom that comes from God above.

As a Marine on Iwo Jima's sands,
    A Flying Tiger in China's skies,
Chasing gunfighters on the owl-hoot trail,
    Your Hollywood star began to rise.

The A-Class films you took by storm,
    Strode through them in cowboy boots,
And won your spurs with crusty John Ford,
    Doing proper Cavalry salutes.

The bad men fell by your fists and Colts,
    And your Winchester, swift and sure,
Evil was properly destroyed in the end,
    And virtue triumphed, clean and pure.

You taught us by action to stand for the right,
    Regardless of how dear the cost,
That compromise is fit for cowards alone,
    And the fight for justice you never lost.

For fifty long years you kept us enthralled,
    With your awesome presence and talent,
And left us inspired with your unique brand,
    Of the American Hero gallant.

By Christine Riker - Jan. 21, 2005

John Wayne

THE STUFF OF LEGENDS

Heroes come and heroes go,
       And only now and then,
Does one become a legend; the rest
       Vanish with the wind.

The mighty hero Beowulf,
       Sprang from Anglo Saxons bold,
The Red Branch Knights of Emain Macha,
       Roamed the Emerald Isle of old.

Good King Arthur had Camelot,
       And his Celtic Knights so pure,
Tales of the Great Round Table,
       And their chivalry long endure.

In Sherwood Forest dwelt Robin Hood,
       And his band of merry men,
Who fought Nottingham's wicked sheriff,
       And brought justice to the glen.

America grew its own brand
       Of hero brave and true,
Neither warrior nor a king,
       But something fresh and new.

He was a common laboring man,
       Who worked astride a horse,
And no one knows quite how he made
       History change its course.

To idolize a hired hand,
       Who rode the range all day,
Driving Longhorns up the Chisholm Trail,
       For very little pay.

The distant mountains were his walls,
       His roof the stars overhead,
A campfire served as dining hall,
       A blanket on the ground, his bed.

Faithful to his saddle pals,
       Few were the words he spoke,
Rode for the brand without complaint,
       His endurance strong as oak.

The "American Cowboy," he was called,
    And his fame spread far and wide,
Through story, novel, song, and film,
    His image would abide.

An independent, resourceful man,
    Who never backed down or quit,
Who conquered every obstacle,
    With dauntless grit and wit.

He came to represent all
    Of man's unending quest,
For freedom which yearned in every heart,
    America at its best.

The twentieth century distilled the tales,
    And bestowed them upon a man,
Who symbolized "The Cowboy,"
    Throughout this hallowed land.

Born Marion Michael Morrison,
    May twenty-six, nineteen hundred, seven,
To Clyde and Mary Morrison,
    Their little gift from Heaven.

But Hollywood gave him to us all,
    And John Wayne will ever be,
The symbol of "The Cowboy,"
    And his "Land of the Brave and Free."

By Christine Riker -05-10-2007

Chris Riker

57

THE MOVIE STAR

He wasn't the most handsome actor in Hollywood,
But to this notion, his adoring fans would never agree,
As the charisma which radiated from his head to his toes,
Made his features seem sublime, for everyone to see.

Until he won his "Oscar" playing a one-eyed marshal,
No one noticed what an excellent actor he had come to be,
Because his mere presence overwhelmed everything else.
Regardless of the role, he was the hero we loved to see.

When boyishly young, playing in his B-class Western films,
He made them so exciting when he appeared in a scene,
Then a war-hero brave, both compassionate and strong,
He made us proud to be Americans on the silver screen.

As a Cowboy, a Soldier, a Firefighter, a Sailor, or a Marine,
He filled each role with integrity and energy to spare,
And made each character he played a man to be admired.
He endowed each one with dignity and dramatic flair.

When we consider the best virtues of the human race,
How to rise above the world's dreary woes and sad despair,
And we search for a hero to show us clearly how it's done.
From his youth to old age, John Wayne was always there!

By Christine Riker
09-19-2019

Chris Riker

5 8

ERMAL AND THE DUKE

Every boy should have a hero,
    And that man should be his dad,
One "greatest guy in all the world,"
    For each and every lad.

God, who made both man and boy,
    Decreed that as His plan,
But somehow things went very wrong
    When Satan tempted man.

So many men refuse the gift
    Of a precious little son,
For lack of which, kingdoms fell,
    When a queen could not bear one.

Such was Ermal Williamson, as he grew
    To manhood on his own,
Without a father's hand to guide,
    He found his way alone.

Fortune smiled and led him to
    A man to be admired,
Bold and tough but always good,
    In cowboy gear attired.

He was called by some, "The Duke,"
    And he knew right from wrong.
A villain never bested him,
    The Duke was big and strong.

He could ride and fight and shoot
    as swift as the western winds.
Bad men were his enemies,
    And good men were his friends.

Heroic deeds in movie films
    Were only make-believe,
But they taught Ermal to be square,
    And never to deceive.

As John Wayne grew into his roles,
    Upon the silver screen,
He became a hero, the likes of which
    The world had never seen.

Actor and hero merged into one,
    And he came to symbolize
America to the entire world,
    Noble, brave, and wise.

Walking in the footsteps of "The Duke,"
    Ermal keeps his name alive,
And reminds us freedom isn't free,
    If America is to survive.

We must fight to uphold the right,
    Just as "The Duke" would have done,
Resist all men who oppress the weak,
    Until justice for all is won.

Three cheers for heroes who blazed the trail,
    Whether real or just "pretend,"
John Wayne, Gary Cooper, Ermal, and all,
    They are our gallant Western men.

By Christine Riker - 10-25-2001

Ermal Williamson is a John Wayne re-enactor
and a published author. After meeting Pilar,
John Wayne's widow, she paid him a
sterling compliment, saying to him,
"You ARE John Wayne."

61

BEN JOHNSON

Across Monument Valley he rode one day,
    In nineteen hundred and forty nine,
Like the champion he was, rode into our hearts.
    A hero that can't be erased by time.

He helped John Wayne look good on the screen,
    As part of that marvelous team,
John Ford's "touring company," they were called,
    As they showed us the Western dream.

They fought through the fearsome Indian Wars,
    McLaughlan, "Dobie", and John Agar too,
Women by their side, they shared their pride,
    With Mildred Natwick and pretty Joanne Dru.

When a lull in the action came about,
    With space and time to fill,
They put Ben Johnson on the back of a horse,
    And galloped him over a hill.

With a band of Indians closing fast,
    Their arrows took deadly aim,
To save the courier in his perilous flight,
    Ben Johnson to the rescue came.

Swift as the wind he rode that day,
    Flung his horse upon the ground,
Astonishing courage to face the foe,
    Defeat was all they found.

And the Yellow Ribbons fluttered still,
    For the Cavalry men in blue,
For Captain Brittles and Trooper Tyree,
    Heroes so fearless, strong, and true.

To the man who was a cowboy born,
    World champion roper by choice,
Stuntman and actor by quirk of fate,
    We raise a grateful voice.

To give him "Thanks!" for all he did,
    What more can mere fans do?
"Hooray!" for the hundreds of roles he played,
    And the Cavalry Trooper in blue.

Chris Riker
3-7-2007

THE BRONC RIDER

In Washington State a boy was born,
  Drew his first breath and began to thrive,
Named Enos Edward by his proud parents,
  In the Year of Our Lord, 1895.

He was riding horses by the time he could walk,
  Entered his first rodeo at age sixteen,
Won the Roosevelt Trophy in Pendleton in 1923,
  That coveted prize, a rodeo cowboy's dream.

He was a famous rodeo star while still in his teens,
  Rode "No Name" in 1920 and "Tipperary" in 1921,
Two notorious "Hall of Fame" buckers,
  A feat no other rider had ever done.

A photographer snapped his picture in 1914, atop a bronc,
  Trying to pitch him through a hole it had kicked in the sky,
Labeled it "Yakima Canutt" and the name caught on,
  And stayed with him until the day he would die.

Hollywood beckoned to Canutt and many other rodeo riders,
  Who, in their off-season, worked as stuntmen and wranglers.
Fate decreed they should meet on some studio back lot,
  There "Yak" and "Marion Michael Morrison" met as strangers.

A partnership was formed...surely one made in Heaven,
  For all who love action on the silver screen,
For Yak and Marion perfected the bar-room fights,
  And made them look real, in every scene.

Yak invented the leap onto the backs of running teams,
  Fell beneath wagons and stagecoaches in flight,
Grabbed the back axles as they passed overhead,
  Giving audiences the world over, nail-biting fright.

Yakima became famous a second time around,
  Doing stunt work for Director, John Ford,
Who taught Marion Morrison to become John Wayne,
  In the Cavalry Trilogy with Winchester and sword.

In 1986 Yakima left us his legacy; a world richer by far,
  In his second-unit directions of Hollywood's best,
From "Stagecoach" to the chariot race in "Ben Hur,"
  By Yakima's life, we have all been blest!

By Christine Riker - 4-11-2015

LIGHTS, CAMERA, ACTION !

Enos Edward Canutt was born in the year eighteen-ninety-five,
Back in the days when the West was still untamed,
In a land as far west as one could find,
For our country's first president, the state was named.

The cowboy life was still in its prime,
Every boy worth his salt could rope and ride,
Enos turned out to be the best of them all,
And its native son filled Washington state with pride.

Enos entered his first rodeo when just a lad of sixteen.
In two short years he was a big-name rodeo star,
Dubbed "Yakima Canutt" by a photographer in 1914,
After snapping his picture on a bronc tossing him high and far.

Yak was a tall, dark, and handsome young man,
A favorite subject of photographers whenever he would ride.
In an era when movie-making was just being born,
Was it any wonder the two worlds would soon collide.

In 1923 in Pendleton, Oregon, he won the Roosevelt Trophy,
Awarded in memory of "Teddy, lover of the sports of range and plain,"
Worth $5,000.00 when a dollar was still worth a hundred cents,
A worthy prize no cowboy would ever disdain.

Wider fame and greater glory was in store for Yak,
For the first movie with a story to tell on the silver screen,
Was a "Western" called "The Great Train Robbery."
Movies now coming of age, cowboys by the dozens could be seen.

Before the advent of sound and "the talkies" were invented,
Wild horse chases and two-fisted action had to tell the story.
Maidens in distress to rescue, and slimy villains to vanquish,
A horseman in a ten-gallon hat was that hero, in all his glory.

The early rough-and-tumble free-for-alls, with its wild thrashing about,
Didn't look quite real to the audience, not totally believable.
Enter young John Wayne, and with the rodeo-star turned stuntman,
They perfected the fights into choreography, very conceivable.

66

No one could ever top the stunts Yak created for the screen,
The hero leaping onto the backs of a running team,
Then falling beneath the pounding hooves and letting go,
To grab the axle of the stagecoach or wagon and upon it swing.

When advancing age prevented him doing dangerous stunts himself,
He became the second-unit director for most of Hollywood's daring-do,
With feats like the great chariot race in the film, "Ben Hur,"
And unforgettable stunts created for John Ford's favorite movie crew.

For all of us who were born in the "Greatest Generation,"
Who spent our Saturday afternoons at the local "picture show,"
Owe our heartfelt thanks and undying admiration,
To you, Yakima Canutt, more than you could ever know.

By Christine Riker - June 12, 2019

THE BOY FROM TEXAS

He played a Cowboy hero, and other roles too,
In Hollywood's land of "lets pretend,"
Brought there by the legendary actor, James Cagney, who,
Seeing his photo on the cover of LIFE, chose to become a friend.

Cagney's movie company never materialized,
But it mattered not at all in the end,
As Universal-International put him under contract,
Thus, his "movie star" status began.

In that tinsel-town land of "make believe,"
He played many roles of heroes bold,
To thrill the Saturday matinee movie goers,
From the very young to the very old.

But this man was no fictitious hero,
From the imagination of script writers on the studio lot,
Because he had lived an adventure in real life,
No writer could have ever created such an unbelievable plot.

Abandoned in childhood by his faithless father,
His mother dying soon after from overwork and a broken heart,
Leaving eleven brothers and sisters to a perilous fate,
A sharecropper's orphan in life, was his heartbreaking start.

Shooting rabbits to feed his hungry siblings,
He dare not miss, for one bullet was all he usually had,
At just age twelve, this was his challenge,
Unbelievable responsibility for such a little lad.

He did not collapse under the crushing load,
For the love of his family he faced the relentless foe,
With courage as great as any hero ever born,
Strong as Sampson, brave as David, Biblical heroes of long ago.

Barely eighteen, soon after Pearl Harbor, he joined the Army,
And sent all his pay home for the children there,
Ordered to the front before he was old enough to vote,
Where terror, bloodshed, and death was the daily fare.

He was awarded twenty two medals for the valor he displayed,
Including the Medal of Honor; the most decorated combat soldier of WWII,
So, when you see him portray a hero on the silver screen,
Know that Audie Murphy's hero status is honorably true.

By Christine Riker   June 7,2019

PORTRAIT OF A HERO

He was born June 20, 1924 to Emmet and Josie Bell Murphy on a sharecropper's farm north of Dallas, Texas, one of twelve children. As a baby, he was strapped in a swing while his mother worked in the cotton fields. From the time he could walk, his life was one of hard work and grinding poverty.

As soon as he could carry a gun, he had to shoot rabbits for the dinner table. Sometimes he could afford to buy only one bullet, so his marksmanship had to be perfect or the family would go hungry. Later, during combat in WWII, that skill would save his life and the lives of his fellow soldiers.

When he was 12, his father deserted the family, leaving Josie and the children to starve. He had to quit school and go to work as a farm hand to support the large family. In 1941, when just 16, his mother died, leaving him to mourn for her the rest of his life. He had to support the large family of siblings alone. The three youngest children had to be put in an orphanage.

The Japanese bombed Pearl Harbor on December 7, 1941, when Audie was 17. On his 18th birthday, June 20, 1942, he tried to join the Marines, but was turned down because he was so thin. Then he tried to join the paratroopers, but was rejected because he was so small. When he tried the Infantry, they let him in. He had never been more than 100 miles from home. He was sent to Camp Wolters, where my two uncles, Floy and Foster Murray, took their basic training. He was so undernourished that in close-order drill, he passed out cold and fell flat on his face. The officers wanted to have him trained as a cook because of his baby-faced youthfulness, but he persisted in becoming a combat soldier. He sent all of his military pay home to support his sisters and brothers, and got the youngest ones out of the orphanage.

He was assigned to Company B, 1st Battalion, 15th Infantry Regiment, 3rd Infantry Division and stayed with that outfit throughout the war. Less than two and a half years later, he was commander of his unit. He contracted malaria in Sicily, which plagued him the rest of his life. War wounds prevented him from going to West Point and becoming a commissioned officer.

Before he was old enough to vote at age 21, after two years overseas, most of it on front line duty, he returned home at the end of WWII with every decoration for valor the United States could bestow: 22 medals, including 3 Purple Hearts, 9 campaign medals, the highest medals France and Belgian could give, and the United States Medal of Honor. Audie Murphy was the most decorated United States combat soldier of World War II.

Audie Murphy was a shy person who shunned attention. James Cagney brought him to Hollywood, where he made his living in predominantly Western movies, until his untimely death in an airplane crash on May 28, 1971. He played the lead in the biographical movie of his life, "To Hell And Back." Unknown to most people, Audie also wrote a number of Country-Western songs and poetry. Here are the poems he wrote in 1948:

POEMS WRITTEN BY AUDIE MURPHY IN 1948.

Dusty old helmet, rusty old gun,
They sit in the corner and wait-
Two souvenirs of the Second World War
That have withstood the time, and the hate.

Many times I've wanted to ask them-
And now that we're here all alone,
Relics, all three, of a long ago war-
Where has freedom gone?

Mute witness to a time of much trouble,
Where kill or be killed was the law-
Were these implements used with high honor?
What was the glory they saw?

Freedom flies in your heart like an eagle,
Let it soar with the winds high above
Among the spirits of soldiers now sleeping,
Guard it with care and with love.

I salute my old friends in the corner.
I agree with all they have said-
And if the moment of truth comes tomorrow,
I'll be free, or by God, I'll be dead!

****

Oh, gather 'round me, comrades; and listen while I speak
Of a war, a war, a war where hell is six feet deep.
Along the shore, the cannons roar. Oh, how can a soldier sleep?
The going's slow on Anzio. And hell is six feet deep.

Praise be to God for this captured sod that rich with blood does seep.
With yours and mine, like butchered swine's; and hell is six feet deep.
That death awaits there's no debate; no triumph will we reap.
The crosses grow on Anzio, where hell is six feet deep.

****

Alone and far removed from earthly care
The noble ruins of men lie buried here.
You were strong men, good men
Endowed with youth and much the will to live.
I hear no protest from the mute lips of the dead
They rest; there is no more to give.

So long my comrades,
Sleep ye where you fell upon the field.
But tread softly please
March o'er my heart with ease
March on and on,
But to God alone we kneel.

AUDIE MURPHY

participated in nine battle campaigns, entitling him to wear nine Bronze Stars (battle stars). He was the most decorated combat soldier of WWII. This is a list of his medals:

MEDAL OF HONOR
Silver Star with First Oak Leaf Cluster
Legion of Merit
Bronze Star Medal with "V" Device and First Oak Leaf Cluster
Purple Heart with Second Oak Leaf Cluster
Good Conduct Medal
Distinguished Unit Emblem with First Oak Leaf Cluster
American Campaign Medal
European-African-Middle Eastern Campaign Medal with One Silver Star, Four Bronze Service Stars (representing nine Campaigns) and one Bronze Arrowhead (representing assault landing at Sicily and Southern France)
World War II Victory Medal
Army of Occupation Medal with Germany Clasp
Armed Forces Reserve Medal
Combat Infantryman Badge
Marksman Badge with Rifle Bar
Expert Badge with Bayonet Bar
French Fourragere in Colors of the Croix de Guerre
French Legion of Honor, Grade of Chevalier
French Croix de Guerre with Silver Star
French Croix de Guerre with Palm
Medal of Liberated France
Belgian Croix de Guerre 1940 Palm

Audie on location in the sand dunes south of Lone Pine, California.

Beyond Glory	1948	Ride A Crooked Trail	1958
Texas, Brooklyn And Heaven	1948	The Gun Runners	1958
Bad Boy	1949	No Name On The Bullet	1959
The Kid From Texas	1950	The Wild And The Innocent	1959
Sierra	1950	Cast A Long Shadow	1959
Kansas Raiders	1950	The Unforgiven	1960
The Red Badge Of Courage	1951	Hell Bent For Leather	1960
The Cimarron Kid	1952	Seven Ways From Sundown	1960
The Duel At Silver Creek	1952	Posse From Hell	1961
Gunsmoke	1953	Battle At Bloody Beach	1961
Column South	1953	Six Black Horses	1962
Tumbleweed	1953	Showdown	1963
Ride Clear Of Diablo	1954	Gunfight At Comanche Creek	1963
Drums Across The River	1954	The Quick Gun	1964
Destry	1954	Bullet For A Badman	1964
To Hell And Back	1955	Apache Rifles	1964
World In My Corner	1956	Arizona Raiders	1965
Walk The Proud Land	1956	Gunpoint	1966
The Guns Of Ft. Petticoat	1957	The Texican	1966
Joe Butterfly	1957	Trunk To Cairo	1967
Night Passage	1957	40 Guns To Apache Pass	1967
The Quiet American	1958	A Time For Dying.....this film never completed.	
		Audie was killed in a plane crash May 28, 1971	

THEIR NAMES WE DID NOT KNOW

Do you remember a time back when,
    A good many years ago,
If our chores were all done and our homework too,
    We could go to see a Saturday picture show?

We loved our heroes one and all,
    And their horses and sidekicks too.
They rode the range and had gunfights,
    And their lives were honest and true.

We knew their names as well as our own,
    And the tricks they did employ,
To save the gal, the ranch, or the town,
    They were Hoppy, Gene, and Roy.

But they couldn't have done heroic deeds,
    Done nothing but ride around,
If nasty, bad hombres hadn't shown up,
    To menace the gal, the ranch, or the town.

We saw their faces each Saturday afternoon,
    Their black moustaches and ominous scowls,
Their skulking walk, their six-guns slung low,
    Cattle thieves, gamblers, and naughty saloon gals.

Glenn Strange played bar-keeps a few hundred times,
    Wiping whiskey glasses by the score,
Roy Barcroft rustled a thousand head of cattle,
    While Pierce Lyden stole a thousand more.

Richard Farnsworth doubled all the stars,
    And he took their dangerous spills,
He made the movies exciting for us,
    With each "shoot-'em-up" full of thrills.

Edgar Buchanan kept the humor at a lively pace,
    And so did our friend, Alan Hale,
Evil Jack Elam with his one crooked eye,
    Cast a wild and scary spell.

Albert Decker was a suave bad man,
    Robert Lowery played a gentleman's game,
With his silver sideburns to distinguish him,
    And John Dehner's voice was his claim to fame.

A bewhiskered old codger was Paul Brinegar,
        Walter Brennan limped through the West,
Big and burley, Mike Mazurki stood tall,
        With Gregg Palmer, Claude Akins, and the rest.

Arthur Hunnicutt added zest to each film,
        And Strother Martin was good as gold,
Royal Dano did acting at its very best,
        In his each and every movie role.

Horses and cows, villains and heroes,
        Were only a part of the scene,
Indians with bows and arrows and feathers,
        Had their place on the silver screen.

Most of the "Injuns" were played by white men,
        Wearing wigs which looked silly and fake,
But it was "make-believe" we all knew,
        And all was filmed for entertainment's sake.

We appreciated the Indians, whether real or not,
        Michael Anasara and Jay Silverheels both,
And Iron Eyes Cody, although his parents were born,
        In Sicily, off Italy's sunny coast.

We saw all their faces on the silver screen,
        'Though at the time, their names we did not know,
We are glad they shared our childhood with us,
        At the Saturday afternoon picture show.

by Chris Riker - October 13, 2011

75

IT TAKES PEOPLE

Alan Ladd riding alone up the valley below the majestic Tetons,
Or Ben Johnson racing across Monument Valley in days of yore,
Filled the screen for a few moments, in the movies of yesteryear,
But to fill the screen for an hour or two, audiences needed more.

A cowboy crew was needed to round up cattle and horses,
A gang of rustlers was needed to rustle them by day or night.
A town was needed as a setting for a bank to be robbed,
A posse was needed to chase the outlaws in their flight.

Actors and actresses filling the screen were varied and colorful.
We remember them as if they were friends, one and all,
Old ones and young ones, like the boys Tommy Rettig and Dick Jones,
Short ones like Elisha Cook, ones like Arthur Hunnicutt, lean and tall.

Memorable are Gunn "Big Boy" Williams, Roy Barcroft, Denver Pile,
Walter Brennan, Andy Devine, Royal Dano, Ward Bond, Walter Reed,
Anthony Quinn, and Chill Wills who always brought a laugh or smile,
And Ken Curtis of "Sons of the Pioneers," a favorite actor, indeed.

Dub Taylor and his son Buck Taylor, Claude Akins, and John Mitchum,
Brother of the famous "Robert," known as "Them Ornery Mitchum Boys,"
Forrest Tucker, Alan Hale, Jr., Mort Mills, Andrew Duggan, Leo Gordon,
And Robert Middleton, those faces as familiar to us as our toys.

They peopled the ranches and towns, they rode in the runaway wagons,
When horses were cut loose, which rolled over the cliffs and crashed.
They rode in stagecoaches when they were held up by the bandits,
They leaped onto villains on horseback, rolled down slopes and smashed.

They tangled in saloon brawls and broke the place to pieces,
Tables, chairs, mirrors, bottles, poker chips, and men went flying,
As stuntmen sailed through break-away windows and bat-wing doors,
And bystanders looked on as gunslingers and victims lay dying.

A sheriff and his posse always headed the outlaws off at the pass,
And we knew the culprits, in their black hats, would be caught in the end,
Because we also knew, without a doubt in our hearts, a cowboy hero,
In a white hat, always came to the rescue. He was our favorite friend.

By Christine Riker 8-21-2019

HORSES, HORSES, HORSES

Where would our movie cowboys have been without their trusty steeds,
The horses we knew and loved as much as we loved our cowboy hero?
The arrival of motor-cars didn't stop them from doing their daring deeds,
Riding tall in the saddle, making sure the villains had nowhere to go.

In early movies Tom Mix had Tony, and Reb Russell's horse was Rebel,
Charles Starrett rode Raider, and Hopalong Cassidy's mount was Topper,
Alan "Rocky" Lane's horse was Black Jack, while Rex Allen rode Koko,
William Elliott had Thunder, and the Lone Ranger saved the day on Silver.

Tex Ritter had White Flash and his comedy side-kick, Slim Andrews,
Amused us with his stubborn mule, Josephine, surely a show stopper.
Eddie Dean changed horses so often they couldn't be counted,
But some of them were War Paint, Flash, White Cloud, and Copper.

The most famous of all, without a doubt, was Gene Autry's horse, Champion,
And Roy Roger's beautiful palomino, the wonder-horse named Trigger,
But the world's favorite cowboy rode any mount available in his B-movie days,
Until John Wayne reached A-movie status, then his favorite mount was Banner.

Western matinee movies were called "Oaters" and "Horse Operas" because
The screen was filled with horses, with some like Trigger, who could dance.
We watched them as they trotted, cantered, and galloped across the landscape,
From Monument Valley to the Alabama Hills and the Corrigan Movie Ranch.

Those were days filled with confidence and hope, days of the cowboy and horse,
When we knew the Black Hats from the White Hats. We knew wrong from right,
Because our Saturday heroes knew what was in "The Good Book" and lived it.
Integrity prevailed, because it was the "Code of the West." We lived in the light.

By Christine Riker - Aug. 17, 2019

THE INDIANS

How could one have played "Cowboys and Indians,"
In childhood days, if no Indians were to be seen?
We had to have them as we created our stories,
Or watched them unfold upon the silver screen.

The enemies were usually bandits and outlaws,
But sometimes they were Indians, fierce and wild,
With a way of life so very different from our own,
They were colorful, even when friendly and mild.

In the old silent movies, real Indians were often used,
But by the 1930s they were mostly replaced by actors,
Who looked so silly in their costumes and fake wigs,
Fooling no one but producers and movie-mogul detractors.

We applaud their efforts to keep us entertained so well,
Whether friend or foe, wherever the storyline did go.
If their skins were dark or painted on, we couldn't tell,
But they were vital to the plot in a Western picture show.

Our hats are off to the actors in the movie-Indians bands:
Michael Dante, Jay Silverheels, Iron Eyes Cody, Chief Big Tree,
Eddie Little Sky, Dehl Berti, Frank DeKova, and X. Brands,
And Michael Ansara, who seemed a real Indian to you and me.

Keith Larson, Graham Green, Wes Studi and Adam Beach,
And even Rock Hudson took his turn playing an Indian part.
Women played Indians as well: Dolores Del Rio, Susan Cabot,
And Debra Paget, added a bit of beauty and a throb in the heart.

Tribes of the Eastern Seaboard: Mohawk, Iroquois, Abenaki, Seminole,
And Cherokee; the war-like tribes of the plains, Cheyenne and Sioux,
Arapaho, Blackfeet-Piegan, Mandan, Ute, Modoc, Pima, and Navajo,
And the fierce Apache and Comanche Tribes, all were given their due.

Some movie stories were real and based on actual history,
Some were fiction and used the names of real people at random.
Screen writers usually played loose and fancy-free with the facts,
Embroidered around the truth with absurd and reckless abandon.

The rest of the world came to view the U.S.A. through "Westerns,"
Whether staying close to reality, or running wild with imagination,
The old black-and-white films of yesteryear, or later in Technicolor,
The "Cowboy Movie" was THE original, authentic American creation.

By Christine Riker 8-21-2019

THE BLACK HATS

The essentials of a movie of any genre, are a hero and a villain.
There must also be a wrong to be righted, and evil schemes must fail.
It helps to have a helpless pilgrim or damsel in distress to save,
And in the end, the hero and righteousness must prevail.

No clearer pattern for a morality play has ever been invented,
Than the Western movies of Hoppy, Gene, and Roy, as the best example.
The Cowboy movies were good vs. bad in bold relief; no in-between,
No gray, no wavering, all was black or white, it was just that simple.

At first, they wore ten-gallon hats with which to water their horses,
And the ladies often wore styles to fit a twentieth-century day.
Horses frequently competed with automobiles while on the roads,
But people who lived before the 1940s, said it often happened that way.

It was usually easy to tell the good guys from the bad guys,
Even when they did not have bandanas covering their ugly faces,
For outlaws mostly wore hats of black upon their heads,
While our heroes wore white hats, as they rode in endless chases.

There couldn't have been a plot in the story without them,
And we knew them almost as well as we knew the cowboy star.
There was the man with the sinister, one-eyed leer, Jack Elam,
Followed by big Jack Palance, whom we recognized from afar.

On both sides of the law, at times, rode Dan Duryea, Victor Jory,
Lon Chaney Sr. and Lon Chaney Jr., Paul Picerni, and Brian Donlevy,
Arthur Kennedy, Greg Palmer, and Mike Moroff, a film star in Mexico,
John Saxon, and Bruce Dern, who played the very meanest "heavy."

John Ireland, Robert Ryan, Ernest Borgnine, and Richard Boone,
Were occasionally the good guys, but more often mean to their bones,
Chris Alcaide, and Pierce Lyden, from the days of the 1930s and 40s,
And recognizable, slant-eyed villains, Lee Van Cleef, and L. Q. Jones.

We give them our heartfelt thanks, along with the rest of the crew,
Black Hats, ladies, side-kicks, horses, the townspeople walking past,
And the bartenders and dance-hall girls who filled the many saloons.
As long as we remember the Westerns, their memory will also last.

They had six-guns that shot non-stop, without ever being reloaded,
Hundreds of bullets hitting nothing but lamps and glasses on a shelf,
Hats didn't fall off in a fight and shirts stayed tucked-in under the belts.
It mattered not at all, it was make-believe; simply for us to enjoy ourself.

By Christine Riker 8-22-2019

Johnny Mack Brown
lays a haymaker on
the villain

The VILLAINS
a k a
The BLACK HATS

Jack Elam
popular villain
of later years

Pierce Lyden
classic Black Hat
of the 1930s and
1940s

Chris Riker

81

HOORAY FOR THE SIDE-KICKS

During the hay-day of Hollywood, its entertainment was varied and vast,
With historical films called "period pieces" and "costume dramas" as well,
Which often took us to another land and a long-ago century in the past,
Having A-class actors, elaborate wardrobes and sets, their stories to tell.

There were films of cops-and-robbers, and a detective called a gum-shoe,
A little terrier named Asta, owners Nick and Nora Charles, "The Thin Man,"
Elliott Ness and the Untouchables who tackled the mobs and Mafia too,
And Boston Blackie and a clever little Oriental sleuth named Charlie Chan.

There were musicals in glorious color, dances with Rogers and Astaire,
Voices of Nelson Eddy and Jeanette MacDonald, to our ears delight,
Pirates ravaging the Spanish Main, spreading terror and despair,
Tarzan swinging through the jungle on vines, in perilous, exciting flight.

Slapstick comedians, The Three Stooges, Red Skelton, and Danny Kaye,
To tickle our funny-bones and leave us rolling in the aisles,
Stingy Jack Benny and the great team, Bing Crosby and Bob Hope,
On the "Roads" with Dorothy Lamour, brought us humor and smiles.

But our favorite movies of all were the "Shoot-'Em-Ups," the Westerns.
How better to spend summer and winter afternoons, to occupy our time.
They taught us right from wrong, self-reliance, honesty, and respect,
At Saturday matinees, all for just two cents, along with one thin dime.

Paul Fix was listed as a character in most of the movies ever made,
Fred McMurray starred in "Smokey," the classic book by Will James,
Even Mickey Rooney wandered out west and danced in mohair chaps,
Comedy was the character actor, Slim Picken's, major claim to fame.

What would our Western heroes have been without faithful side-kicks,
To lighten life with humor and laughter, and help them out in a pinch,
As did Richard "Chito" Martin with the handsome, boyish Tim Holt,
And with Jimmy Ellison on the Bar-20, Hopalong's heroics was a cinch.

At the Lone Ranger's side was "Tonto," played by Jay Silverheels,
Tex Ritter had Slim Andrews, whose mule, Josephine, drug him in the dirt,
We laughed at George "Gabby" Hayes, who mistrusted all the women-folk,
And Smiley Burnett's antics as Frog Millhouse, kept Gene Autry alert,

Remember Russell Hayden, Pat Buttrum, Fuzzy Knight, Walter Brennan,
Al "Fuzzy" St. John, and so many more, who helped as supporting actors,
And the bands, often in the background, but at times up front and center,
The Cass County Boys and Sons of the Pioneers; all were important factors.

By Christine Riker 8-23-2019

Hooray for the Side-kicks, whose antics made the movies such fun to watch.

George "Gabby" Hayes

Lester Alvin "Smiley" Burnette

Chris Riker

John Forrest "Fuzzy" Knight

Jeremiah Schwartz
aka Andy Devine

HOORAY for the SIDE-KICKS

Biographical tidbits.

George "Gabby" Hayes: Born May 7, 1885 in Wellsville, New York, was the lovable, laughable, side-kick in over 200 Westerns. He began his career in vaudeville, entering films in the 1920s. He played villains in some early John Wayne movies. In the 1930s, he began playing the side-kick to Western stars, especially William Boyd and Roy Rogers. Typically he was a toothless, bewhiskered, fearless old-timer who distrusted all women-folk. In the 1950s, he had his own television show. Undoubtedly, he is the most well-known of all the Western side-kicks.

Smiley Burnette: Born Lester Alvin Burnette on March 18, 1911, in Summum, Ill. A talented musician and comic, he appeared on radio and in vaudeville after graduating from high school. He appeared with Gene Autry on the National Barn Dance, then they both entered films in 1934. Between 1935 and 1942, they appeared together in 81 films, with him playing Gene's comic side-kick, "Frog Millhouse." He appeared in 200 Westerns, with such screen partners as Allan "Rocky" Lane, Sunset Carson, and Charles Starrett. He wrote over 300 songs, many of which were used in his movies. From 1964 to 1967, he appeared in the TV series "Petticoat Junction."

Fuzzy Knight: John Forrest Knight was born May 9, 1901, in Fairmont, West Virginia. He began his career as a musician, singer, and bandleader in nightclubs and in vaudeville, before entering films as a comic. He played in more than 200 Westerns, as a side-kick to Tex Ritter, Johnny Mack Brown, and other Western heroes. He occasionally played straight dramatic roles.

Andy Devine: Born Jeremiah Schwartz, on October 7, 1905, in Flagstaff, Arizona. He was a football star in his college days. He arrived in Hollywood in 1926, playing bit parts in silent films. His raspy voice, which was the result of a childhood accident, became an asset when he was typecast as a country bumpkin and comic side-kick for Roy Rogers and other Western stars. He played in numerous B and A films, and after television came along, he played "Jingles," the side-kick of Guy Madison in the TV series, "Wild Bill Hickok," in the 1950s. He later starred in his own series, "Andy's Gang." He served for several years as honorary mayor of Van Nuys. Perhaps he is best remembered as the stagecoach driver in John Wayne's "Stagecoach" in 1939.

Slim Andrews: Born Lloyd Andrews on December 8, 1906 in Gravette, Arkansas. His movie career was as the side-kick to Tex Ritter. Tex landed his first part on Broadway and in films in 1930. Tex was a Grand Old Opry headliner, as well as a collector of genuine cowboy ballads. He was the only entertainer to be elected to the Cowboy Hall of Fame and the Country Music Hall of Fame. In 1940, they began touring coast to coast with their mounts, White Flash and Josephine. During that time, I saw them in person on stage, in the little theater in Gorman, TX. Josephine was on stage with Slim, but White Flash didn't accompany Tex that particular day. Slim's mother lived in Sulphur Springs, near Gravette, and attended the same Baptist church which my parents attended in the late 1950s, after they moved from Texas, during a severe 10-year drought. In those days, preachers habitually referred to actors and actresses as adulterers and adulteresses. One Sunday morning Mrs. Andrews could stand no more. She stood up, addressed the minister, and told him in no uncertain terms, that her son Slim was not an adulterer, but was a fine Christian gentleman, and not to ever call him a "Hollywood adulterer" again. I dare say, he never made that mistake again.

DAMSELS - IN - DISTRESS

It may have become tiresome and boring for our cowboys bold,
If all they had to do was chase horses and cattle all day long,
Or rescue ranches and towns from outlaws, in those days of old,
So, the singing cowboy was added, with a western song.

Singing to no one but his horse while in the saddle all day,
Or bedding the herd down for the night, under a silver moon,
To calm the restless critters so they wouldn't wander or stray,
Singing to the cattle calmed them, so the night rider would croon.

Soon ladies were added to the story, bringing beauty and a smile,
And they could be rescued too, along with all others in dire need,
As they cringed in helpless fear of the villains, mean and vile,
But were saved in-the-nick-of-time by the cowboy's heroic deed.

Republic Studios had its crew of lovely damsels-in-distress,
Adrian Booth, Peggy Stewart, Elaine Riley, and also Ruth Terry.
Ann Rutherford, who received her first film kiss at age eighteen,
From Gene Autry, but as he was married, she said it felt a bit scary.

Beautiful Anne Jeffreys, who starred with a young Robert Mitchum,
In his first starring role, a Western, "Nevada," filmed at Lone Pine,
Lois Hall, Gail Davis, and Marie Windsor, who starred both in B-films,
And A-films, and who played with John Wayne three times.

We remember most of all, Dale Evans, who rode the silver screen,
With Roy Rogers, King of the Cowboys, in real life and on TV,
Idols of childhood for three generations, because they were good,
Actors, singers, parents, Christian leaders, heroes we loved to see.

Poverty Row studios gave us good entertainment for the 12 cents
We spent for a ticket at the Saturday matinee when we were young,
Then major studios got in on the act and added its own bright stars,
Like Rita Costino, who later became Rita Hayworth, added to our fun.

They gave us such beauties as Maureen O'Hara and Joanne Dru,
Yvonne DeCarlo, Paulette Goddard, Susan Hayward, Virginia Mayo,
Anne Francis, Gail Russell, Loraine Day, and Barbara Stanwick, too,
Arlene Dahl, Rhonda Fleming, and actress turned director, Ida Lupino.

Little girls played "Cowboys and Indians," just as well as the boys.
We felt for the long-suffering damsels-in-distress, in those days of yore,
And believed within our hearts, when we grew up to be the ladies,
A cowboy hero would appear and rescue us, and would be ours forevemore.

By Christine Riker 8-20-2019

Some of Republic Studio's B-Western movie heroines, those "damsels in distress," who needed a dashing cowboy hero to rescue them and set everything right by the end of the movie.

Ann Rutherford was a star in A-movies, as well as the B-movies. She was Scarlett's sister in "Gone With the Wind." Her very first kiss, at age 18, was from Gene Autry, at the end of a Saturday matinee movie.

Peggy Stewart's experience with Gene Autry was when he and Champion leaped over her in her convertible automobile.

Peggy Stewart

Ann Rutherford

I attended the ceremony on Oct. 10, 2013, in Lone Pine, CA, when Peggy and Loren Janes were given their Lifetime Achievement Awards.

Frances Octavia Smith was a successful radio and night-club singer, before becoming the "Queen of the West," and the partner and wife of Roy Rogers, the "King of the Cowboys."

She was late for the event, and Loren quipped, "Peggy is always late."

Adrian Booth

The Cupid's Bow lips, and bright red lipstick, dates these damsels to the 1940s.

Dale Evans

Ruth Terry

Damsels in the Saturday Western =matinee movies were not always in this much distress, but they still appreciated a handsome cowboy hero coming to their rescue.

THE STUNTMEN

Western movies were action films, first and foremost,
Action was more important than dialogue or indoor scenes,
Physical fitness in the movie stars was a prerequisite,
Strength as important as handsome faces, for the movie screens.

Some Western stars could have, and a few occasionally did
Their own stunts, but it was not the rule. Common sense prevailed,
Insurance companies forbid it, the studios could not afford it,
If a leading star was injured, or Heaven forbid, accidentally killed.

Stuntmen became very necessary, to protect the producers,
The studios, the investors, and the actors and stars, as well,
There were no computers faking reality back in those days,
Real people did stunts so expertly, that audiences couldn't tell.

When a stuntman or woman was injured or killed during filming,
It was quietly kept under wraps and was never publicized,
To protect the reputations of the studios and the industry,
And to keep stuntmen and women from being demoralized.

The most famous stuntman of all, was the cowboy, Yakima Canutt,
Who taught John Wayne the choreographed art of throwing a punch,
Without really touching the villain, while they tore the place apart,
Thus uninjured and best of friends, they could sit down for lunch.

My heroic friend, Loren Janes, who was twice an Olympic champion,
Was Steve McQueen's career double; once doubled Debbie Reynolds too.
Dean Smith, the other Olympic champion, born in Breckenridge, Texas,
Near my home County of Eastland, we give praise and thanks to you!

These stuntmen deserve our utmost respect and admiration,
Because they risked their lives daily, to give us those exciting thrills,
Which made the Western movies we loved to see so interesting.
They took the bruises, falls, hits, crashes, the dangers and the spills.

Neil Summers; Whitey Hughes; Richard Farnsworth and his son, Diamond;
Jack Williams; Roydon Clark; Robert Hoy; and the daring Dar Robinson,
Rex Rossi, who doubled Bob Steele in so many "Oaters" of 1940s movie days,
And our favorite star, John Wayne's loyal double, the great Chuck Roberson.

By Christine Riker 8-23-2019

STUNTMEN

Fred Graham

Yakima Canutt

Chuck Roberson
who was
John Wayne's
stunt double

Dean Smith

Chris Riker

Whitey Hughes

89

THE UNSUNG HERO

Do you remember way back when
        We were young in years,
And life was made of school and play,
        And yet untouched by tears?

Evenings spent by the radio,
        Gave us childish joy,
With Terry and the Pirates and Jack Armstrong,
        The All-American boy.

But Saturdays were the best of all,
        For that was when we'd go
To "Butter and Egg Day" in the town,
        And see a picture show.

Twelve cents bought a whole new world,
        So different from the farm,
Handsome heroes, brave and bold,
        Who saved the world from harm.

There were cartoons and a one-reel-short,
        A mystery and sneak previews,
A cliff-hanging serial and a shoot-em'-up,
        And the latest Movietone news.

Mysteries were solved by detectives sly,
        The inscrutable Charlie Chan,
Boston Blackie and Sherlock Holmes,
        And Nick Charles, the suave Thin Man.

But the movies that we liked best,
        Were the Western ones, of course,
With our dashing cowboy heroes,
        And their side-kick and their horse.

They were always straight and true,
        And they kept us glued to our seats,
As we watched in admiration and awe,
        While they did their thrilling feats

There was Hopalong Cassidy and Johnny Mack Brown,
    And Gary Cooper, the quiet cowpoke,
And that cantankerous old Gabby Hayes,
    Who mistrusted all women-folk.

Trigger was our favorite horse,
    And we loved Roy Rogers too,
And liked to hear Tex Ritter sing,
    When the long day's work was through.

Tonto was the Lone Ranger's friend,
    He was loyal and true,
And gravel-voiced Andy Devine was there,
    A saddle pal we all knew.

We howled with mirth at Frog Millhouse,
    And all his funny antics,
And wondered how our Cowboy could
    Avoid the gal's romantics.

Gene Autry strummed his sweet guitar,
    Serenading a pretty Miss,
But it was against the Code of the West,
    To think of stealing a kiss.

Action was what we went to see,
    None of that mushy stuff,
Ridin' and ropin' and horses and cows,
    And men who were rawhide tough.

Cowboys who leaped on horses with ease,
    From the rear with a single bound,
Sprang into their saddles from balconies high,
    And never fell off on the ground.

When a team ran away with wagon or coach,
    They leaped onto the churning mass,
Dropped down beneath the pounding hooves,
    Grabbed an axle as it rolled past.

They jumped from swiftly running steeds,
    Knocking outlaws from their saddles,
With two-fisted punches put an end
    To the culprits futile battles.

Without reloading even once,
        Colts blazed like shooting stars,
In ambush, duels, Indian fights,
        And old-time cattle wars.

They saved the damsels in distress,
        Townsfolk and settlers too,
Kept the ranches from being foreclosed
        When the mortgages came due.

We knew the names of our cowboy stars,
        And their side-kicks and horses too,
But unknown to us were the men who helped
        Make our Saturday dreams come true.

They were the unsung heroes
        Who brought excitement to the screen,
Who gave us daring spills and thrills,
        In a West we had never seen.

Bold Yakima Canutt started it all,
        With nerve and courage to spare,
He taught the Duke how to fight,
        With conviction and comic flair.

Followed by stuntmen like Loren Janes,
        A man devoid of fear,
Who created spectacular action scenes,
        In his profession he has no peer.

They rode across a make-believe range,
        John Wayne and Randolph Scott,
In a gun-smoke haze, our hum-drum days,
        Each Saturday, we soon forgot.

As we settled down in a theater dark,
        Transported to a distant past,
To our grandfather's day when the West was young,
        To a time that couldn't last.

Until those men on the silver screen
        Brought the West to life once more,
Where it will stay, undimmed by time,
        American's Cowboy lore.

By Christine Riker - 10-01- 2001

Loren Janes created and executed the major stunts in "How The West Was Won," including the spectacular cactus scene. When the movie premiered in France, the audience gave this scene a standing ovation.

Loren, a former mathematics teacher, gymnast, and twice an Olympic Champion, was the stunt double for Steve McQueen during Steve's entire career.

Below, Loren is hanging above Chicago's L-Train, without any safety equipment, using only his gymnastic skill and strength, in this scene...

...from McQueen's last film, "The Hunter."

Chris Riker

an older Loren Janes

FAREWELL TO A HERO

On October 1, 1931, a man-child was born in Sierra Madre, CA.
He entered this world the way all baby boys do,
But God had plans for this special little lad,
And would guide and protect him his whole life through.

Both triumph and tragedy enveloped his world,
In a most unusual and extraordinary way,
Thus, developed a man of heroic proportions,
Whom we gather to honor on this special day.

High adventure was in his heart and soul, right from the start.
He won every blue ribbon in swimming at the local YMCA,
When he was just a little boy at the tender age of seven.
He wasn't interested in the usual games children play.

Between the ages to ten and seventeen, he became a real-life "Tarzan,"
Named himself "White Otter," and left behind his home,
Wearing only a breechcloth and carrying nothing but a hunting knife,
Hiked the 220-mile John Muir trail, four times, all alone.

At Cal Poly the awards he achieved in athletic events during the 1950s,
Could fill a book, they are far too many to name.
He was the first civilian in the Modern Pentathlon in the Olympics,
In 1956 and again in 1964, for Loren, another claim to fame.

Bereaved of his father when he was a lad of only thirteen,
A Marine killed in action on Guadalcanal's bloody shore.
Loren followed in his dad's footsteps by becoming a Marine,
And added to his luster in the Korean War.

Serving under the "Marine's Marine," the legendary "Chesty" Puller,
Loren broke and held the record on the obstacle course,
Fired expert with pistol and rifle, setting the 1000 meter record prone.
In martial skills, to be reckoned with, Loren was a force.

A Renaissance Man to the very core, there was nothing Loren could not do,
A scientist in Biology, Plant and Animal Ecology, played the French Horn.
An opera singer, a tenor, horseman, bow-hunter, scuba-diver, surfer, ski instructor,
Movie photographer, film lecturer, and an adventurer, natural born.

A single parent who raised his two children, Eric and Erica, from ages six and eight,
He was devoted to helping youth and raised vast sums of money for their cause.
Became the most famous stunt-man in Hollywood history, rivaling Yakima Canutt,
A gymnast unmatched by anyone, he continued as he aged, without a pause.

He famously dove into the movie and television stuntman's business,
With an eighty foot dive off a cliff at Catalina Island in an Esther Williams film,
Becoming a real-life hero by saving two other divers who would have drowned,
When they were knocked unconscious and unable to swim.

Loren went on to do stunts and play in thousands of movies and television shows,
So many it would take hours to recite just a few.
He doubled every major actor in Hollywood, he was in most of the famous movies,
And dressed in wigs and skirts, he doubled for the ladies too.

For Steve McQueen's entire career, he owed his "cool" to Loren Janes,
Who made the actor look so good in every dangerous situation,
From his car chase in "Bullitt" on San Francisco's hills,
To "Nevada Smith's" cattle stampede, way out on location.

Loren was the consummate pro who planned his stunts with all the skill
And precision he had used as a high-school teacher in Science and Math.
He seldom was injured and never broke a bone in all those years,
Saving the studios millions of dollars, deterring many a director's wrath.

Loren invented the most famous stunts Hollywood ever enjoyed,
Since Yakima Canutt drug under the stagecoach's flying wheels.
Loren leaped onto that saguaro cactus from the speeding train,
Played Debbie Reynolds falling from a wagon and taking to her heels.

Loren won every prestigious award Hollywood had to give,
So many they filled the walls of his Angeles National Forest home,
The Golden Boot, the Silver Spur, and Lone Pine's Lifetime Achievement too.
He earned his rest, to settle down in his old age, and never more to roam.

Loren was co-founder of the Stuntmen's Association of Motion Pictures & Television,
The very first stuntmen's organization. His affiliations were too many to list.
He was fiercely patriotic and a devoted Christian. He was more than just a man,
He was the stuff of heroes, the stuff of legends, and he will be sorely missed.

Loren and his lovely wife, Jan, lost their home to the Sand Fire, July 23, 2016,
In that wild conflagration. Life is both joy and grief, without reason or rhyme.
Loren embarked on his greatest adventure on June 24, 2017, when his Master called,
And the man, the hero, became a legend for us and a legend for all time.

Loren's achievements seem too awesome to be real, so surely they must be
Some Hollywood writer's fanciful fiction, thus his legend will grow.
But we who knew and admired this man who was flesh and blood, heart and soul,
Bid farewell to a friend, not to a legend, and each of will know...

The time will come when we will join our friend in his great adventure,
And in that day how joyful it will be,
To share once more the love we knew while here on earth with Loren,
In never ending peace and glory, for all eternity.

By Christine Riker July 9, 2017

Loren Janes and Chris Riker, Sonora, CA 2001

Loren and wife, Jan Sanborn, a concert pianist .

On location in Lone Pine, CA, Loren shows locations where he rolled down the hillside in a wagon, played both settlers and Indians being shot, and doubled for Debby Reynolds when she fell out of the wagon, in the great movie, HOW THE WEST WAS WON.

LOREN JANES

Chris Riker 2004

97

ENTER THE RE-ENACTORS

After the era of the movie Westerns, the old black-and-white Saturday matinees,
The Cinemascope epics with major stars like Gary Cooper and Clark Gable,
And the great "Trilogy" collaboration of the John Ford "touring company,"
A treasure-trove of the great John Wayne, until he was old and almost feeble.

Television caused the glory-days of the Western movies to wane,
Then television Western programs took their place on a little screen,
They too began to cease, with a generation which only looked forward,
To computerized films of outer space, aliens and demons weird and mean.

To save our Western screen history, some brave men took up the challenge,
And became both movie and TV star re-enactors, to their loyal fans delight,
They join the ranks of Cowboy idols we want to remember, entertaining us,
At Western Film Festivals, until time also fades them away, into eternal night.

Our thanks to Don Shilling, aka "Paladin"; who hired his gun to serve justice,
Ronnie Aycoth, who took the role of Bill Elliott, "Red Rider" and "Wild Bill,"
Joe Sullivan, aka "Hopalong Cassidy" and Harry Dunkle, aka "Charles Starrett."
And Jake Thorn, aka, "John Wayne," at Lone Pine, out in the Alabama Hills.

By Christine Riker 8-24-2019

Re-enactor.
Joe Sullivan as
William Boyd,
aka - Hopalong Cassidy

Re-enactor, Ronnie Aycoth as
William Elliott, aka Red Ryder
and Wild Bill Hickok

Re-enactor posing as the Lone Ranger. His identity is a secret.

Re-enactor, Ermal Williamson, aka John Wayne. Wayne's widow, Pilar, after meeting Ermal, told him, "You ARE John Wayne

Re-enactor, Jake Thorne aka John Wayne

Re-enactor, Harry Dunkle, aka Charles Starrett.

Re-enactor Dan Shilling, aka Richard Boone, aka Paladin .

THEN ALONG CAME TELEVISION

After WWII came to an end, the Allies having won that ghastly war,
Everything changed, including Hollywood; then we began to see,
Film Noir, dark and gloomy; no longer the light fare we saw before,
The stories where right triumphed over evil, almost ceased to be.

On the horizon loomed "television," a new-fangled technology,
At first called a "vast wasteland" as it adjusted to what was in store,
As it slowly felt its way to programming for a new audience,
And how to change its format; could it copy things that went before?

While both A-and B-class actors felt their future shrouded in mystery,
The Saturday matinee Westerns, and the big-budget Westerns galore,
Were to much a part of the American culture, heritage, and history,
To be left behind in the dust-bin, or abandoned on the cutting room floor.

So a new genre entered the picture, quite literally, on the "small screen,"
With a new crop of actors, because at first, the "big screen" personnel
Felt it beneath them to humble themselves and let themselves be seen,
On a medium, which to them seemed to be their career's death-knell.

Not to be deterred, the geniuses in the show-business industry,
Put on their thinking-caps and came up with a brilliant plan,
To create Western programs which would fit a 30-minute time frame,
And save the Cowboy-Hero image of the western working man.

Thus the national television network, known to the world as NBC,
Picked up the apt and dubious nickname of "Nothing But Cowboys."
Some programs were entertaining, like "Bonanza," "The Big Valley,"
And "Little House On The Prairie," but some were only boring noise.

But they helped save the Western too; we will give them their just due,
And although their names don't rhyme, let us give them ample time:
Dale Robertson; Clint Walker; Fess Parker; James Arness; Peter Graves;
Ken Curtis; James Drury; Doug McClure; James Garner; and Jack Kelly;

Jock Mahoney; Hugh O'Brien; Forrest Tucker; Guy Madison; Duncan Regehr;
Chuck Connors; Loren Green; Michael Landon; Dan Blocker; Will Hutchens;
Bruce Boxlietner; Kenny Rogers; Neville Brand; Kelo Henderson; Jack Lord;
Clu Gulager; Barry Sullivan; Jeffrey Hunter; Lee J. Cobb; and Harry Lauter;

Earl Holliman; Robert Conrad; Ross Martin; Lee Majors; Richard Long;
Jim Davis; Guy Williams; Robert Fuller and John Smith of "Laramie" fame,
Ty Hardin; John McIntire; Dennis Weaver; James Garner; Ward Bond;
And the two scouts, Robert Horton and Denny Miller, on "Wagon Train."

By Christine Riker 8-23-2019

Then Along Came Television

James Drury
as
"The Virginian"

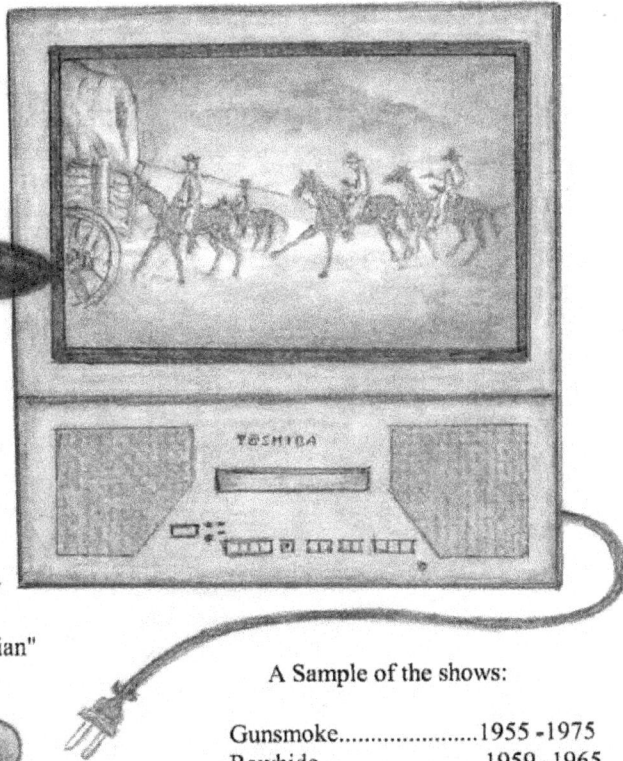

A Sample of the shows:

Gunsmoke......................1955 -1975
Rawhide........................ 1959 -1965
Bonanza ....1959 -1973
Maverick........................1957 -1962
The Lone Ranger.............1949 -1957
Have Gun-Will Travel.....1957 -1963
Wanted: Dead or Alive....1958 -1961
Wagon Train....................1957 -1965
The Rifleman...................1958 -1963

Dan Blocker as the beloved
brother, Hoss Cartwright, in
"Bonanza."

Chris Riker

101

THE TEXAS RANGERS

Had there never been a TEXAS, the "Cowboy Culture" would not be.
While the men were away serving their country during the Civil War,
From the Sabine to the Rio Grande, Longhorn cattle roamed wild and free.
Railheads to ship the cattle were in Kansas, if critters could walk that far.

Thus, the great cattle-drives and famous cattle-trails of the west began,
Forming the basis for stories, songs, poems, and movies by the score.
The "Cowboy" became a legend in his own time; a western working-man.
The vast, rugged landscapes of the west, fixed its location forevermore.

But the beginning of TEXAS had its start many long decades before,
When Mexico invited frontiersmen from the U.S.A. to settle on the land,
As a buffer against Plains-Tribes living there, the Apache and Comanche,
Whose fierceness had prevented expansion. Would colonists lend a hand?

Mexico gave land-grants to settlers from Scotland, Germany, and others,
But most famous was the colony of three hundred families from the U.S.A.,
Led by Stephen F. Austin, in 1821, to the south-central part of the land,
Content to build log cabins, till the soil, and raise their children day-by-day.

Understandably, the warrior-tribes of the Plains Indians felt threatened,
By the increasing number of Anglo-Americans arriving day and night,
Disturbing their ancestral hunting grounds and the game and buffalo.
The incompatibility their of ways-of-life soon led to a life-or-death fight.

Mexico had separated itself from Spain and flew its own flag by 1824.
Under its banner Anglos arrived and thrived, until a power-hungry dictator,
Santa Anna, seized control of the nation, attacking several of its states,
Including Texas; but freedom-loving Anglos refused to be a mere spectator.

General Sam Houston led the rag-tag Texans to victory at San Jacinto,
After the fall of the Alamo in San Antonio, and its thirteen days of glory.
Thus, Texas became a sovereign nation in 1836, for ten troubled years,
Until joining the U.S.A., an integral part of the whole Western story.

The earliest settlers on that wild and dangerous frontier needed help,
Needed it desperately, to protect their new homes and families dear,
From depredations and murder-raids by ferocious Comanche bands,
While plowing fields, rifles leaning against nearby fences, out of fear.

Armed groups of men from settlements and ranches came together,
To protect the small, vulnerable towns, as well as each isolated farm,
From Indian raids and bandits, on both side of the border, because,
There was no military or law-enforcement to protect them from harm.

Continued:

Texas needed men who were practical and suited to conditions in the wild,
Alert to every event, ready to adapt to each immediate, dire situation,
So they chose a man to lead them and went forth to engage in battle.
The problem solved, each man returned home to resume his occupation.

The first use of the word "Ranger" occurred in the year 1823, when
Stephen F. Austin hired ten men to serve, at his own, personal expense,
As Rangers; an irregular militia without uniforms or military structure,
Because the colonies were in desperate need of a dependable defense.

The following century brought about a wide variety of service,
Although there was no permanent, well-recognized Corps at first,
Each Ranger supplied his own horse, equipment, knives and guns.
Known for their bravery and skill, often honored, sometimes cursed.

Their exploits became so notoriously famous and world-renowned,
It was inevitable they should become the subject of song and story.
They didn't disband or fade away when Texas joined the United States,
But became a permanent police force, adding to their luster and glory.

Such names come to mind, as the Frontier Battalion, and the Salt War,
The Cortinas War on the Rio Grande, Col. Samuel Colt and his gun,
The Colt Walker, developed for the Rangers, so they would have a chance
Of having equal firepower with the Comanche warriors on the run.

So many famous names associated with the Texas Rangers, we recall,
Like L. H. McNelly; Captain Wm. Eastland, and Captain John Coffee Hays,
The famous Frank Hamer, who took down the outlaws, Bonnie and Clyde,
And notorious bad-men like the bandit Sam Bass, in the "olden days."

Now the Rangers have a permanent headquarters in Waco, Texas,
Along the Brazos, one of many Texas rivers flowing down to the Gulf.
The phrase, "One Riot, One Ranger" comes to mind, adding to their fame,
Showing the world that the Texas Rangers are made of "the right stuff."

Little wonder then, that Hollywood studios came knocking at their door,
"The Texas Rangers," with Fred McMurray; Lloyd Nolan; Jack Okie in 1936,
Remade as "The Streets of Laredo," starring Wm. Holden; Wm. Bendix;
And MacDonald Carey in 1949. Then along came television with a new fix.

TV shows included "Tales of the Texas Rangers," filmed back in 1955,
With Harry Lauter and Willard Parker, alternating modern stories with old;
"Laredo," with Neville Brand and Phillip Carey, and my favorite in 1993,
"Walker, Texas Ranger," with Chuck Norris; thus the Ranger's story was told.

By Christine Riker - 8-25-2019

Not the glamorized movie or television Texas Rangers, but the real thing. Four Texas Rangers along the Texas-Mexico border, which was swarming with bandits, hostile Indians, rustlers, and villains of every description before and after Texas won her independence from Mexico in 1836.

Left to right: Pete Crawford, Ray Miller, John Poole, and Arch Miller.

OUT OF THE REVOLUTION

The stars have gleamed with a pitying light
On the scene of many a hopeless fight,
On a prairie patch or a haunted wood
Where a little bunch of Rangers stood.

They fought grim odds and knew no fear,
They kept their honor high land clear,
And, facing arrows, guns, and knives,
Gave Texas all they had - their lives.

By W. A. Phelson

To learn the history of the Texas Rangers, read "The Texas Rangers" by Walter Prescott Webb, the University of Texas Press, Austin, Texas - Copyright 1935 and 1965.

The REEL Texas Ranger
vs
The REAL Texas Rangers

Captain L. H.
McNelly

Captain Frank Hamer

Captain Ben McCulloch

Captain
W.J.
(Bill)
McDonald

CHUCK NORRIS
AS

Colonel John
Coffee Hays

WALKER
TEXAS RANGER

Major John S. (RIP) Ford

Chris Riher

COWBOY CODES, CREEDS, AND PRAYERS

In today's culture, 2019 A.D., as this book of Cowboy lore is being written, the so-called entertainment industry, including video-games, television programs, and movies, are teaching the public to accept violence, killing, greed, immorality, sloppy, outlandish attire and hair, and mutilation of the body, as normal behaviors.
They are not.

In the days of the Saturday matinee, the 1930s and 1940s, the entertainment industry consisted of books, radio programs, and the movies. They taught the public that "in the end, morality, righteousness, and justice always prevail."

The battles of our heroes of yesteryear, such as "Hoppy, Gene, and Roy," reinforced the teaching that "righteousness over evil" is the correct way to live.

The following are their Creeds:

GENE AUTRY'S COWBOY CODE OF HONOR

1. The Cowboy must never shoot first, hit a smaller man, or take unfair advantage.
2. He must never go back on his word or a trust confided in him.
3. He must always tell the truth.
4. He must be gentle with children, the elderly, and animals.
5. He must not advocate or possess racially or religiously intolerant ideas.
6. He must help people in distress.
7. He must be a good worker.
8. He must keep himself clean in thought, speech, action, and personal habits.
9. He must respect women, parents, and his nation's laws.
10. The cowboy is a patriot.

HOPALONG CASSIDY'S CREED FOR AMERICAN BOYS AND GIRLS

1. The highest badge of honor a person can wear is honesty. Be mindful at all times.
2. Your parents are the best friends you have. Listen to them and obey their instructions.
3. If you want to be respected, you must respect others. Show good manners in every way.
4. Only through hard work and study can you succeed. Don't be lazy.
5. Your good deeds always come to light. So don't boast or be a showoff.
6. If you waste time or money today, you will regret it tomorrow. Practice thrift in all your ways.
7. Many animals are good and loyal companions. Be friendly and kind to them.
8. A strong, healthy body is a precious gift. Be neat and clean.
9. Our country's laws are made for your protection. Observe them carefully.
10. Children in many foreign lands are less fortunate than you. Be glad and proud you are an American.

WILD BILL HICKOK DEPUTY MARSHAL'S CODE OF CONDUCT

1. I will be brave, but never careless.
2. I will obey my parents. They DO know best.
3. I will be neat and clean at all times.
4. I will be polite and courageous.
5. I will protect the weak and help them.
6. I will study hard.
7. I will be kind to animals and care for them.
8. I will respect my flag and my country.
9. I will attend my place of worship regularly.

THE LONE RANGER CREED

1. I believe that to have a friend, a man must be one.
2. That all men are created equal and that everyone has within himself the power to make this a better world.
3. That God put the firewood there, but that every man must gather and light it himself.
4. In being prepared physically, mentally, and morally to fight when necessary for that which is right.
5. That a man should make the most of what equipment he has.
6. That "this government, of the people, by the people, and for the people," shall live always.
7. That men should live by the rule of what is best for the greatest number.
8. That sooner or later...somewhere...somehow...we must settle with the world and make payment for what we have taken.
9. That all things change, but the truth, and the truth alone, lives on forever.
10. I believe in my Creator, my country, my fellow man.

ROY ROGERS RIDERS CLUB RULES

1. Be neat and clean.
2. Be courteous and polite.
3. Always obey your parents.
4. Protect the weak and help them.
5. Be brave but never take chances.
6. Study hard and learn all you can.
7. Be kind to animals and care for them.
8. Eat all your food and never waste any.
9. Love God and go to Sunday School regularly.
10. Always respect our flag and country.

ROY ROGERS PRAYER

Lord, I reckon I'm not much just by myself,
I fail to do a lot of things I ought to do.
But Lord, when trails are steep and passes high,
Help me ride it straight the whole way through.
And when in the falling dusk I get that final call,
I do not care how many flowers they send,
Above all else, the happiest trail would be
For you to say to me, "Let's Ride, My Friend."

Amen.

TEXAS RANGERS "DEPUTY RANGER'" OATH

1. Be alert.
2. Be obedient.
3. Defend the weak.
4. Never desert a friend.
5. Never take unfair advantage.
6. Be neat.
7. Be truthful.
8. Uphold justice.
9. Live cleanly.
10. Have faith in God.

CREED OF THE TEXAS RANGERS

"No man in the wrong can stand up to a man in the right who just keeps on a-comin'"

JOHN WAYNE - AMERICA'S COWBOY - HIS CODES

As he embodied them in his movie roles and lived them in his personal life.
Some of his wit, wisdom, and advice - embodying the honesty, loyalty, grit, and
the unwavering values of the America he loved and the image of the American Cowboy.

1. All battles are fought by scared men who'd rather be someplace else.
2. Bravery is being scared to death but saddling up anyway.
3. Just give the American people a good cause, and there's nothing they can't lick.
4. John Wayne's spoken-word album, "America, Why I Love Her," written by another
   movie actor, John Mitchum, the not-quite-as-famous brother of Robert Mitchum.

AMERICA, WHY I LOVE HER

You ask me why I love her? Well, give me time, and I'll explain...
Have you seen a Kansas sunset or an Arizona rain?
Have you drifted on a bayou down Louisiana way?
Have you watched the cold fog drifting over San Francisco Bay?

Have you heard a Bobwhite calling in the Carolina pines?
Or heard the bellow of a diesel in the Appalachia mines?
Does the call of Niagara thrill you when you hear her waters roar?
Do you look with awe and wonder at a Massachusetts shore...
Where men who braved a hard new world, first stepped on Plymouth Rock?
And do you think of them when you stroll along a New York City dock?

Have you seen a snowflake drifting in the Rockies...way up high?
Have you seen the sun come blazing down from a bright Nevada sky?
Do you hail to the Columbia as she rushes to the sea...
Or bow your head at Gettysburg...in our struggle to be free?

Have you seen the mighty Tetons?...Have you watched an eagle soar?
Have you seen the Mississippi roll along Missouri's shore?
Have you felt a chill at Michigan, when on a winters day,
Her waters rage along the shore in a thunderous display?
Does the word "Aloha"...make you warm?
Do you stare in disbelief when you see the surf come roaring in at Waimea reef?

From Alaska's gold to the Everglades...from the Rio Grande to Maine...
My heart cries out...my pulse runs fast at the might of her domain.
You ask me why I love her?...I've a million reasons why.
My beautiful America...beneath God's wide, wide sky.

THE WESTERN

The first feature film ever made was a Western, "The Great Train Robbery."
    It was the first movie to have a plot and tell a story, starting a new tradition.
Now, even those who could not read or write, the illiterate and the children,
    Could see a story without having to read it or hear it orally, by recitation.

The movie industry and Hollywood were birthed early in the 20th century,
    Only a short time after the real Western frontier began fading into the past,
So important a part of history could not be allowed to die... it must be saved,
    In music and song, story and books, in paintings and on film, so it would last.

We pay tribute to the early pioneers of "Cowboy" films, those so soon forgotten,
    By new generations who don't know the value of learning from the past.
We remember the cowboys of the silver screen, thrilling us with their daring-do,
    Real cowboys turned reel cowboys, teaching us that justice will triumph at last.

Indians, heroines, villains, horses, cattle, stuntmen, Cavalry men, and pioneers,
    Directors and producers, writers and cameramen, all too numerous to mention,
Engineers who invented the cameras and wranglers who tended the livestock,
    They all learned how to please the audience and get our undivided attention.

We are told a person never really dies as long as his name is remembered,
    So let us do our part, keeping their names alive for our children and posterity.
The names of those Cowboy actors who thrilled us so much, as we were growing up,
    Will not be erased by "space-age heroes" and fall into dusty obscurity.

Broncho Billy Anderson	Rod Cameron	William S. Hart	Ken Maynard
Don"Red" Barry	Sunset Carson	Monte Hale	Col. Tim McCoy
Rex Bell	Lane Chandler	Jack Holt	Tom Mix
Monte Blue	Ray Corrigan	Tim Holt	Robert Montgomery
William Boyd	Jim Davis	Jack Hoxie	Clayton Moore
Johnny Mack Brown	Richard Dix	Buck Jones	George O'Brien
Harry Carey, Sr.	Hoot Gibson	Tom Keene	Bob Steele
Harry Carey, Jr.	Raymond Hatton	Lash La Rue	Max Terhune

All the "A" class stars did at least a few Westerns. These are some of our favorites:

Dana Andrews	Henry Fonda	Brian Keith	Tyrone Power
Charles Bronson	Glenn Ford	Bert Lancaster	Ronald Reagan
Gary Cooper	Clark Gable	Joel McCrea	Jimmy Stewart
Kirk Douglas	Sterling Hayden	Steve McQueen	Robert Taylor
Preston Foster	Charlton Heston	Robert Mitchum	Spencer Tracy
Errol Flynn	William Holden	Gregory Peck	Richard Widmark
Clint Walker	Robert Preston	Alan Ladd	Dennis Weaver

After the "Golden-Age-of-Hollywood" ended, a decade of poorer quality Westerns followed, and the so-called "Spaghetti-Westerns" with Clint Eastwood. Afterward, directors such as Simon Wincer and Robert Totton directed good Westerns with new stars:

Tom Selleck - Sam Elliot - Robert Duvall - Tommy Lee Jones - Tom Berenger

I saw movies starring Johnny Mack Brown, William Boyd, Bob Steele, Charles Starrett, Gene Autry, and Roy Rogers when I was a child. Richard Dix, Hoot Gibson, Buck Jones, Col. Tim McCoy, Harry Carey, Sr., and Tom Mix were all a bit before my time. Earlier pioneers were William S. Hart, William Farnum, and Broncho Billy Anderson. We are grateful to each and every one of them for helping to preserve the Western legend for the enjoyment of our generation, as we were growing up.

Hoot Gibson

Buck Jones

Johnny Mack Brown

Tim McCoy

Bill
Boyd
as
Hopalong
Cassidy

Tom Mix

Tom Mix was Hollywood's first stuntman. (1880 - 1940)

Richard Dix

111

EPILOGUE

At Western Film Festivals and Cowboy Poetry and Music Gatherings, I've heard a poem which asks, "Whatever Happened to Hoppy, Gene, and Roy?" In essence, the question is, "Whatever happened to virtue, honesty, loyalty, purity, courage, and conscience?" These were the codes the Western movie cowboy lived by, but by the latter part of the twentieth century, they had vanished from American culture. By 2020, even common civility is in short supply. The Cowboy Code was, of course, based on Judeo/Christian culture, which had been a civilizing influence for the past 2,000 years, lifting our western civilization out of its barbaric, pagan roots. As given to mankind in the Holy Bible, the basic code of conduct is called The Ten Commandments. The Ten Commandments, Cowboy style are:

1. Just one God
2. Honor y'er Ma and Pa
3. No tellin' tales or gossipin'
4. Get yourself to Sunday meetin'
5. Put nuthin' before God
6. No foolin' around with another feller's gal
7. No killin'
8. Watch y'er mouth
9. Don't take what ain't y'ers
10. Don't be hankerin' fer y'er buddy's stuff

The iconic Cowboy movie hero wearing a white hat, doing battle against vile villains, coming to the rescue of anyone in danger or need, can be best summed up by the career and private lives of Roy Rogers and Dale Evans. This is the testimony of some folks who were influenced by them:
"Roy Rogers and Dale Evans are every bit the heroes America and the movies made of them. To me, they stand as the example of the best things to come out of Hollywood."
Clint Black, country-western singer-songwriter

"He used his immense talent to encourage moral and spiritual strength. Roy Rogers took the best of America's most important icon, the Cowboy, and created a code of honor for all. He was the most important American entertainer in the twentieth century."
Michael Martin Murphy, country-western singer-songwriter

"Today there are movies and television shows that I wouldn't even let my horse Trigger see. Kids still like to see the good guy win and the bad guy lose. When the roles are reversed, as in many of today's movies, kids get their thinking in trouble."
L. A. Daily Times, interview with Roy Rogers. September 15, 1976

As my friend in the movie industry, Loren Janes, and Ben Johnson, told me, Hollywood was just an ordinary place to work during its Golden Age, but not after the 1960s when the "hippie-drug culture" took it over. The great actor, Joel McCrea said, before passing away in 1990, that now Hollywood was producing filth. What happened? America rejected the Biblical-based laws and civilization given by the Founding Fathers and followed Europe in its return to paganism and man-centered idolatry.

In our imaginations, we dream of a hero, such as the Lone Ranger, coming to our rescue, riding on a magnificent white horse. Is there yet any hope for us? Yes! GOD, (Father, Son, and Holy Spirit) who created everything in the universe, including cows, horses, and cowboys, must have a special place in his heart for the cowboy. Why do I think this? He sent His Son, Jesus, to take our punishment and die on a cross on Cavalry so that by accepting His Gift, we will have eternal life when we leave this body which was created for life on earth. The ultimate Hero, Jesus Christ, is coming to the rescue of mankind, at the appointed time, riding on a white horse, to vanquish and destroy the ultimate villain, Satan, who created all the harm, sorrow, illness, and death on earth. Will he be wearing a white hat? Who knows...but on his clothing will be written, "King of Kings, and Lord of Lords. *Rev. 19:11-16.*

Christine L. Riker